3.50

# Energy in Evolution

This pioneering study of Teilhard de Chardin's concept of hyper-physics (which he believed would be 'the physics of the future') represents an attempt to look at the 'within' as well as the 'without' of things at every level, to bring together mind and matter, and to relate the facts of natural science with those of religious experience.

The key sentences of this book are to be found in the first chapter, in which the author states emphatically that hyperphysics does not represent "just another reconciliation of Christian faith and the theory of evolution", but rather "a theory based on empirical evidence which leads to conclusions which are similar to the tenets of the Judaeo-Christian religion."

ENERGY IN EVOLUTION is worthy of close study, as Bernard Towers mentions in his Preface, by all who are concerned with thinking, and with the role that thinking might play in the future evolutionary development of man.

# THE TEILHARD STUDY LIBRARY

*General Editors*

ANTHONY DYSON
*Principal of Ripon Hall, Oxford*
BERNARD TOWERS
*Fellow of Jesus College, Cambridge*

# ENERGY IN EVOLUTION

John O'Manique

HUMANITIES PRESS
New York          1969

First published in the U.S.A. in 1969 by
HUMANITIES PRESS, New York, N.Y.

Printed in Great Britain

# Contents

*Foreword*


The writings of Teilhard de Chardin are marked by a constant and passionate concern for man and his future. They show throughout a great faith in man, and a conviction that mankind, which he sees as an organic and self-organizing whole, has before it prospects full of promise. This conclusion was in no way the result of facile optimism. It sprang instead from a sustained effort to understand the coherence that exists between the Christian doctrine of creation and redemption on the one hand and, on the other, our modern scientific insight into man as the product of, and participant in, a remarkable evolutionary process. Teilhard concluded that man must no longer be thought of as a passive observer of evolution, but rather as an active agent prolonging and developing this world-in-process into a future where the full dimensions of personhood can be realized in and by every individual.

In no sense did Teilhard claim to provide a detailed blue print for the construction of the future. Rather, he sought to explore and to expound a coherent way of seeing man-in-society-in-nature-in-evolution. He wanted others to take up, correct and enrich his own ideas. He also welcomed the fact that others would set themselves to the same task independently of his own ideas, from different starting-points and by different means.

Thus, in *The Teilhard Study Library* we are not concerned so much to add to the growing corpus of exposition and commentary on Teilhard's ideas as to publish the work of scientists, theologians and others who, whether or not directly influenced in their thinking by Teilhard, nevertheless share his belief in the urgent need for man to find significance in the cosmos and to develop a common humanist credo. For it is by an "ascent towards the personal" in all states and conditions of human existence, that we act out our responsibility for building the earth.

*General Editors*

ANTHONY  DYSON

BERNARD  TOWERS

Other volumes in *The Tielhard Study Library* are listed opposite the title page, and further books are in preparation.

*Preface*

by

Bernard Towers

In this last third of the twentieth century science and technology have reached a critical stage of development. It looks as if, before the year 2,000, one of three possibilities is likely to ensue. (1) The current 'drift' from science on the part of the young might reach landslide proportions. Increasing discontent and disillusionment with the 'affluent society', to which modern scientific and technological methods have given rise, might put an end to the Age of Science, which would fade away as other 'ages' have done in the past. (2) The next possibility is that scientific achievements might proceed as before and at an ever-increasing pace, with the possible result that catastrophe might overtake what has already been called our "runaway world". It is probable that it is this very fear of possible catastrophe ahead that lies behind the current rejection of science by many of the younger generation. (3) But as a third possibility, man might finally learn how to live with the scientific knowledge he has acquired; he might learn how to control technology in a way that would not only improve the existing benefits (and they are very real ones) that science has brought, but would also satisfy his deepest aspirations for the common good at a much higher than purely material level.

There are many signs within science that the old exclusiveness, separatism and specialization are things of the past. All over the world scientists are meeting not only together and in interdisciplinary groups, but also with philosophers, theologians and other exponents of the 'humanities', to examine afresh the social, political, psychological and even spiritual implications of their work. Man is looking afresh at himself, at his place in nature, and indeed at nature itself, in an

ix

attempt—groping and hesitant though it must necessarily be—to integrate his experience of himself, as being both part and product of the evolutionary process, in a way that makes sense.

The present volume represents a significant contribution to this exploratory movement. The author began his career with degrees in physics and mathematics, and he includes an accurate statement of the way of thinking about physical energy that has dominated western thought for over a century. Modern research physicists, and astronomers who work at the frontiers of knowledge about the physical nature of the universe, may no longer concern themselves with the implications of the laws of classical physics when applied (or misapplied) on a universal scale.[1] Yet there can be no doubt that the mental picture of a universe in which only one kind of energy is recognized (and that of a kind thought to be 'running out') has been something of an obsession with literary authors in recent decades, as well as with orthodox biologists brought up on reductionist philosophy and the nineteenth century 'billiard-ball' hypothesis of the nature of matter.

From physics Dr. O'Manique moved to academic philosophy, and wrote his doctoral thesis on "The Theory of Orthogenesis in the Synthesis of Teilhard de Chardin". He now holds the post of Associate Professor of Philosophy in St. Patrick's College, Ottawa. He spent the year 1966-7 on sabbatical leave in the Department of the History and Philosophy of Science in the University of Cambridge.

His exposition of Teilhard's concept of hyperphysics, and his analysis of the relations between this new discipline and the older ones of physics and metaphysics, will repay close study by all who are concerned with *thinking*, and with the role that thinking might play in the future evolutionary development of man. If physics and metaphysics were characteristic products of the static world of the past, hyperphysics is the unifying science of a world 'on the move'. The volume here presented is inevitably exploratory, and its conclusions will surely be modified in the light of future studies. This is typical of all honest studies of the modern world by 'modern' men. However strange might appear some of the conclusions at first reading, the author's integrity and his intellectual rigour should ensure that no-one will content himself with a single reading of the book.

[1] See Saslaw, W., in *The Teilhard Review*, Vol. 3, no. 2, Winter 1968-9, pp. 76-79.

# Introduction

The name of Pierre Teilhard de Chardin is known to millions. The rate at which his works are being consumed by an audience with widely divergent interests testifies to his phenomenal popularity and broad appeal. It seems, however, that many of his vast following have not approached a true understanding of his synthesis. His theory is both comprehensive and profound, and even scholars who take profundity in their stride have difficulty in grasping the extensive unity of Teilhard's thought. There is a natural tendency to categorize his work into traditional compartments,—to judge it as if it were natural science, or philosophy, or theology. It is in part all of these; but as a whole it is none of these. Teilhard says that it is *hyperphysics;* that is, a new science which is based on, but extends beyond, natural science, and is, moreover, a replacement for metaphysics.

Hyperphysics is based on natural science in that it develops from accepted scientific theories, especially the theory of evolution. Its object is the whole man within the context of an evolving universe, and consequently hyperphysics goes beyond the traditional limits of natural science by looking at the within of things (consciousness) as well as the without (complexity). In so doing hyperphysics develops into a synthesis which is at once scientific and philosophical, and, in its discussion of the future of man, moves into the domain of natural theology.

It is no wonder then that Teilhard's synthesis is difficult to comprehend. The use of esoteric language and concepts of modern science presents an obstacle that the non-scientist may not easily hurdle, and Teilhard's own sometimes poetic style and coined terminology add to the difficulties.

One of the purposes of this work is to try to make hyperphysics more accessible to more of those who are interested in Teilhard. To this end we will (especially in Chapter I), look at some of the scientific theories upon which hyperphysics is grounded to give the reader a glimpse of the scientific world-vision within which Teilhard worked. An understanding of his synthesis demands that we, to some extent, see the dynamic and continuously developing universe that Teilhard, the working palaeontologist-geologist, saw.

To introduce the second, and possibly more important, purpose of this work we will recall the words of the General Editors of this series in their Foreword to Volumes One and Two. They point out that, "Teilhard de Chardin never claimed to have constructed a closed and definitive system of thought which would be protected and propagated after his death by 'disciples'." They say further that, "Teilhard attempted to sketch the provisional outline of a synthesis which would integrate the Christian Gospel with the evolutionary self-consciousness of modern man—an outline which he hoped others, from many different starting points, would correct, develop and apply."

This work is not intended to be simply an exposition of hyperphysics. It is an interpretation of some aspects of the theory and an analysis of some of the major problems. More specifically: in Chapter II we will present an interpretation of Teilhard's concept of energy. The concept of energy is fundamental and essential in hyperphysics, and yet was left somewhat vague and undeveloped by Teilhard. Our interpretation, therefore, goes beyond Teilhard's own words; nevertheless we hope that it might be Teilhardian.

In Chapter III we will look briefly at Teilhard's theory of evolution as a development of complexity-consciousness; but, since this theory is discussed at great length by Teilhard we will concentrate most of our attention in this chapter on two major problems which arise out of it: the problem of orthogenesis and the problem of entropy.

Chapter IV ventures (not too far) into the question, "is hyperphysics scientific?" We do no more than introduce the problem by looking at some aspects of Teilhard's thought in the light of the criteria for good science.

I have kept in mind the fact that this volume is a part of a "study series". If it leads to further study, then, it will have, to that extent, fulfilled its function. Teilhard's work is so extensive, involving the whole spectrum of science, philosophy and theology in one way or other, that its proper evaluation and development would require the work of specialists in many fields. One, therefore, becomes involved in hyperphysics with some hesitation and trepidation. I am somewhat encouraged to hear Teilhard say: "It is very much better to present tentatively a mixture of truth and error than to mutilate reality in trying to separate before the proper time the wheat from the chaff. I have followed without hesitation this Gospel rule which is the rule of every intellectual endeavour and of all scientific progress."

Some material from my articles in *The Teilhard Review* (Volume 1, Number 2 and Volume 2, Number 1) has been used in this volume.

John O'Manique

CHAPTER ONE

# The Genesis of Hyperphysics

"My only aim in these pages—and to this aim all of my powers are bent—is to see; that is to say, to develop a homogeneous and coherent perspective of our general extended experience of man. A whole which unfolds."[1]

This quotation, taken from Teilhard's foreword to THE PHENOMENON OF MAN, which he entitled 'Seeing', is much more than a statement of Teilhard's aims. It is also an indication of his attitude towards the world and the method he uses to fulfil his goal.

The emphasis on seeing in this quotation, and throughout the whole foreword, introduces us to Teilhard the empirical scientist. Teilhard's work as a palaeontologist and geologist depended upon his ability to see and to interpret what he saw. And what he saw in the geological layers through which he excavated, and from which he extracted, measured and classified fossils, presented Teilhard with a part of the coherent picture of man which he sought. Other parts of this picture were provided by the various other branches of the natural sciences, and as a result Teilhard's concept of man is based on what we might call a 'scientific world vision'. To understand Teilhard therefore, one must, to some extent, share in Teilhard's "world vision" as a natural scientist.

Teilhard's total concept of man, however, is not based upon his world vision as a natural scientist alone. He believed that it is possible for natural science to see more than it has seen in the past. "The time has come," he said, "to realize that an interpretation of the

[1] THE PHENOMENON OF MAN, p. 35.

universe—even a positivist one—remains unsatisfying unless it covers the interior as well as the exterior of things; mind as well as matter. The true physics is that which will, one day, achieve the inclusion of man in his wholeness in a coherent picture of the world."[1]

The total picture of man can, then, be seen within physics, or better, within the natural sciences. But not within physics as it exists today. The natural sciences must be extended to encompass not only the exterior of things, which can be directly sensed, but also their interiority. It is this extension of physics that Teilhard refers to as hyperphysics. In order to understand Teilhard's hyperphysics then, it is necessary not only to share in his world vision as a natural scientist but also to have some grasp of his "extended world vision". We shall begin now with some discussion of Teilhard's view of the universe as a natural scientist, and then proceed to its extension into hyperphysics.

## TEILHARD'S SCIENTIFIC WORLD VISION

The world vision of the modern natural scientist is radically different from the world vision of the layman, or what we might call the 'common sense world vision'. A simple example will illustrate this point. Without the assistance of scientific theory or apparatus, the desk in front of me appears to be a smooth, flat, solid, hard surface. It seems to be composed of densely packed matter;—so densely packed that from my vantage point I can see no possibility of anything sifting through it. This, however, is not the way a physicist as a physicist sees it. He may view the surface of this desk as a swarm of sub-atomic particles, or packets of energy, with relatively immense distances between them, moving with very high velocities. He may picture a book resting on the desk not as one body in contact with another, in the traditional common sense of the word 'contact', but as the interaction of two force fields. The two views are decidedly different, and consequently, statements following from the scientific point of view may make no sense at all unless the point of view is understood.

As mentioned before, Teilhard was a geologist and palaeontologist. His doctoral thesis, written under Boule at the Sorbonne, was on the mammals of the lower eocene period in France, and won high praise from his examiners. Although a member of the Jesuit order,

[1] *Ibid.*

Teilhard lived and worked as a professional scientist in his chosen field. He gained wide acclaim and respect as a natural scientist and to verify his productivity as a working scientist, one need only look through the long list of his publications in his bibliography.[1]

As a palaeontologist and geologist, Teilhard worked within the context of the modern theory of evolution; and it is this theory which forms the basis of his 'scientific world vision' and consequently, of his hyperphysics. It is this theory, therefore, that we will now discuss.

The essence of Teilhard's synthesis is contained in THE PHENOMENON OF MAN and THE PLACE OF MAN IN NATURE. The manuscript for the former was completed in 1938 and permission to publish the latter work was sought in 1950. Three of the theories which form a basis of the evolutionary view of the universe were presented before these dates. Charles Darwin's THE ORIGIN OF SPECIES, in which the development of living things was explained in terms of natural selection, was published in 1859. In 1927, Canon Georges Lemaitre proposed a theory to explain the origin of the universe, derived from an application of Einstein's theory of relativity. In 1936, the Russian scientist Oparin published his theory on the origin of life, providing a connecting link between the other two theories, that is, between the physical development from the elements to the heavy molecules, and the biological development of living species.

Darwin, Lemaitre, Oparin, and all their successors who are still developing these theories, have presented to science the basis of its new world vision: a vision of the world as a continuously developing, dynamic, homogeneous unit,—a world, as Darwin expressed it, in which from so simple a beginning, endless forms most beautiful and most wonderful have been and are being evolved. Because of their importance to Teilhard's world vision, the theories of the origin of the universe, the origin of life and Darwin's theory of evolution will be discussed briefly.

THE ORIGIN OF THE UNIVERSE

The most widely accepted theory of the origin of the universe is a

[1] Cf. "Bibliography of the Works of Teilhard de Chardin" in Cuénot, TEILHARD DE CHARDIN, Helicon, Baltimore, 1965. (Original French text by Plon, Paris, 1958.)

B

development of Canon Georges Lemaitre's "Evolutionary Universe", or "Big Bang" theory. According to this theory, the universe was born in a tremendous explosion of energy which produced vast amounts of hydrogen, which is the simplest element and constitutes more than 95% of our physical universe. Helium and the other elements gradually developed from hydrogen. As this material rushed out from the centre of the explosion, gravitational forces eventually brought about the formation of the galaxies, and then, within the galaxies, the star systems with their planets evolved.[1]

A second theory, which is now losing support, is the 'steady state' theory of the universe. The name comes from its premise (based on the red-shift in the spectrum of distant galaxies) that the universe is expanding, but the density of any large volume remains constant. This steady state of density is maintained by the continuous creation of hydrogen.

From the point of view of the evolution of elementary matter, the difference between the two theories lies in the explanation of the manner in which the fundamental building block, that is, hydrogen, is produced. Apart from the origin of hydrogen itself, there is basic agreement on the development of more complex matter from hydrogen. Accordingly, either theory presents a view that the physical universe has developed continuously from the simplest elements of matter to its present state.

THE ORIGIN OF LIFE

It is generally accepted today that a development in complexity on the inanimate level can occur, that is, that a development from the simplest elements, hydrogen and helium, to the most complex molecules such as protein and nucleic acid can come about in nature. Such development is relatively well understood by the physical chemist and the organic chemist, and can be duplicated by them in the laboratory. Next to the origin of the elements which make up the universe, the second critical point in the scientist's explanation of the history of the universe is the origin of life. In the last twenty years, however, much of the mystery which surrounded this problem has been dissipated and it

[1] Cf. Gamow, "Modern Cosmology", in SCIENTIFIC AMERICAN, March 1954. For evidence that Teilhard favours this theory Cf. THE PHENOMENON OF MAN, pp. 47 and 49.

is generally accepted today that living forms did naturally evolve from the non-living.

There is evidence that the transition from the heavy molecules, in particular protein and nucleic acid, to living organisms is both continuous and natural, just as is the transition from atoms to molecules. The discovery and analysis of the virus has especially strengthened the theory of the origin of life. First, the virus has a peculiar combination of living and non-living characteristics. Like a living thing it can reproduce with inheritable changes and it metabolizes. In fact, it is the product of its metabolism which causes disease. Unlike living organisms, however, it does not respire and, more strikingly, it can be crystallized, stored for an indefinite period, and does not lose its infective powers. Finally, it can be broken down into non-living protein and nucleic acid and then resynthesized to an active virus. Viruses, then, are on the borderline between the living and non-living. Although modern viruses are parasites, it is believed that free-living viruses may have existed and indeed could have been the intermediate between non-living and living beings millions of years ago.

Life as we know it today requires four basic classes of compounds: nucleic acids, proteins, carbohydrates and fats. Nevertheless, recent research has shown the protein and nucleic acid to be so fundamental that they may be considered to be the basic minimum of life. Nucleic acid forms the basis of reproduction, and proteins, as enzymes, are the major factors of metabolism or growth. To illustrate the role of nucleic acid and protein in living organisms we will look briefly at the chemistry of chromosomes.

The chromosome is the carrier of the cell's heredity and the guide of the organism's development. The chromosome contains deoxyribonucleic acid and ribonucleic acid, commonly referred to as DNA and RNA. DNA is the actual genetic or hereditary substance.

DNA is in the form of two long, helically coiled, intertwined chains, composed of a sugar and a phosphoric acid joined together by hydrogen bonds. The bonds are nucleotide bases: adenine, guanine, cytosine, and thymine. Referring to these by their initials, A always pairs with T, and C with G. In cell division the DNA ladder splits and each C attracts a new G and vice versa; and each A attracts a new T and vice versa, thus forming two similar ladders (and also similar to the original) excluding accidents. This then is the basis of reproduction.

B1

As stated above, the protein is the basic element in metabolism or growth. In the human body there are between 10,000 and 100,000 different proteins. They are made of about twenty different amino acids in long chains coiled in various and complicated ways. The genetic message encoded on the DNA in the form of a sequence of A, T, C, and G is translated by means of RNA into the sequence of the amino acid "letters" in a chain composing a certain protein.

Even an oversimplified explanation such as this indicates the complexity of these fundamental processes. It would appear at first sight that such complexity could never have developed naturally; but although science has not yet been able to duplicate the whole process synthetically in the laboratory, certain parts of the process have been developed in this way. We mentioned above, for example, that the virus has been resynthesized; that is, the living virus has been broken into its components, nucleic acid and protein, and then the nucleic acid and protein have been reunited to form a living virus.[1] The now famous experiment of S. L. Miller is worth mentioning as a further example of the synthesis of the complex fundamentals of life in the laboratory. It is believed that the primeval earth was covered with a hot, near-boiling ocean rich in methane and ammonia, and subjected to electrical discharges from continual thunderstorms. These conditions were duplicated in the laboratory by Miller and amino acids, the basic component of the protein molecule, were produced. This strengthens the possibility that, in the environment of the early earth, the molecules of protein and nucleic acid may have developed and primitive life itself may have been naturally synthesized.

In summing up we may say that research into the cell and its components shows on the one hand the vast complexity of the fundamental constituents of life, but on the other hand, also shows the possibility, or indeed the probability, of this complexity having developed naturally from very simple physical components, such as water, ammonia, and methane.

DARWIN'S THEORY OF EVOLUTION

We have followed the theoretical history of natural development from its beginnings in elementary energy or particles, up to the origin of

[1] Recent reports indicate that a synthesis of viral deoxyribonucleic acid (DNA) has been achieved in the laboratory.

life. From this point, development is explained in terms of the century-old Darwinian theory of evolution. The basic Darwinian principles of the prodigality of nature, variation and natural selection, are still generally accepted by the scientific community. The modern theory of the chromosome adds to the Darwinian explanation of variation. Before continuing with a brief explanation of this theory, we must make a distinction between evolution itself and the method whereby things evolve. That the creatures in existence on earth today have evolved from lower forms is most probable, indeed so probable that, for all practical purposes, it may be considered to be a fact. The exact method of evolution is not as certain and in discussing Darwin's theory we will be presenting the explanation of the method of evolution that, according to the criteria for good theories, must be considered the most probable explanation.

Returning to Darwin's principles: the prodigality of nature and variation are directly observable. With regard to the former, it is known that many more organisms are born than can possibly survive to maturity. For example, if all the offspring and their descendants of two starfish lived long enough to reproduce normally, in fifteen generations there would be $10^{79}$ starfish. Ten to the seventy-ninth power is the estimated number of electrons in the visible universe. Under the same conditions the elephant, possibly the slowest breeder on earth, would produce nineteen million descendents from one pair in about seven hundred and fifty years. This fact of the prodigality of nature, coupled with the fact of variation (i.e., the fact that no two living beings, even if they are offspring of the same parents, are exactly alike), led Darwin to his theory of natural selection. Variation within a species causes various degrees of adaptability to the environment. The organisms with "good" characteristics, that is, characteristics that are compatible with their surroundings, will more probably survive long enough to reproduce. As we move along the scale in the descending order of good characteristics, the organisms will have less and less chance to survive long enough to reproduce. Certain characteristics, then, will be more or less favoured and therefore more or less likely to be passed on to the next generation. Given enough time, and the geologist and physicist tell us that there was enough time, the changes will be great enough to give rise to what is called a new species. In Darwin's time the problem was: what causes variation, and how are changes transmitted? The Mendelian laws of heredity and the discovery of mutations have solved much of this problem.

There is, therefore, the possibility, indeed for most scientists today, the probability of a continuous evolution of inanimate beings from the simplest to the most complex, a natural transition from the inanimate to the animate, and then a continuous development of animate beings from the simplest forms such as the virus to the most complex forms, the modern primates. (The order Primate includes tree shrews, lemurs, tarsiers, monkeys, the anthropoid apes, and man.)

The fossil record of man is far from complete. There is, however, much evidence of a gradual evolution from a more primitive ape-like body up to and including modern man (homo sapiens sapiens). From Dryopithecus of the pliocene period, through Australopithecus, the Pithecanthropus group, Neanderthal man, Cromagnon (an early form of modern man), to modern man himself we see a gradual transition of physical features which can best be explained if we accept the gradual evolution of the present human body from a more primitive ape-like form.

In the light of all these theories, namely the theory of evolution, the theory of the origin of life, and the theory of the origin of the universe, the scientist views the world as a continuously developing, dynamic process. It is no longer viewed as a static, compartmentalized world composed of beings which were substantially finished by the act of creation, composed of unchangeable essences, and unbridgeable specific differences, but rather as a mutually interacting, homogeneous becoming. This is the world vision of the scientist, and it is the world vision of Teilhard the scientist; it is from this world vision that his synthesis flows. It is only within the context of this world vision that his theory can be understood. In his introduction to THE PHENOMENON OF MAN, Sir Julian Huxley attached special importance to this point: "In THE PHENOMENON OF MAN he has effected a threefold synthesis—of the material and physical world with the world of mind and spirit; of the past with the future; and of variety with unity, the many with the one. He achieves this by examining every fact and every subject of his investigation sub specie evolutionis, with reference to its development in time and to its evolutionary position . . . His . . . perhaps most fundamental point is the absolute necessity of adopting an evolutionary point of view."[1]

We cannot over-estimate the importance of this view of

[1] Huxley, in: THE PHENOMENON OF MAN, pp. 11 and 12.

reality as a continuously developing, dynamic, interacting process. Teilhard was interested primarily in man, and it is within this context that he sees man, and attempts to shed more light upon the nature of man and the future of man. Any analysis of man as he exists here and now, and any forecast of the future of man must recognize the total human context in time and space. It must, in other words, be based on the general theory of evolution which, says Teilhard "is a general condition to which all theories, all hypotheses, all systems must bow and which they must satisfy henceforward if they are to be thinkable and true. Evolution is a light illuminating all facts, a curve that all lines must follow".[1]

It is obvious, then, that Teilhard's own theory, the hyper-physics which we are going to discuss in this work, is based upon the general theory of evolution. It flows, therefore, not from any one science, but from all the natural sciences: from the accounts of the origin of the universe found in cosmogeny, physics and astronomy; from the accounts of molecular development and the origin of life found in physical chemistry, organic chemistry and biochemistry; from the account of the evolution of living organisms found in the various branches of biology; and from the accounts of the origin of man himself as found in anthropology and in Teilhard's own special field of palaeontology.

Teilhard, of course, was not a specialist in all of these fields. He did have, nevertheless, a good understanding of the theories of evolution at both the physical and biological levels; and, more important, as a paleontologist, directly and professionally concerned with a certain section of the evolutionary process itself, Teilhard possessed that kind of feeling and insight into evolution that only a working, experimental scientist could possess.

TEILHARD'S TOTAL WORLD VISION

It is not within the context of the theory of evolution alone that Teilhard sees man. The limits of his world vision are not defined by the natural sciences. Teilhard was not only a natural scientist, but also a Christian, and as a result he saw man not only in the context of evolution, but also in the context of the Divine Milieu, and his aim

[1] THE PHENOMENON OF MAN, p. 218.

was to show that these two contexts were in reality one;—to present a truly Christian view of God, and Man's union with God, based upon scientific theory, while avoiding a dualism of matter and spirit, of body and soul.

Teilhard's total world vision then, encompasses and unites the dynamic evolving universe of the natural scientist and the spiritual universe of the believing Christian. He does not, however, base his hyperphysics upon his Christian beliefs; the concepts of God or Immortality are not among the premises of hyperphysics. Nor is hyperphysics just another reconciliation of Christian faith and the theory of evolution. It is, as we hope to show to some extent, a theory based on empirical evidence which leads to conclusions which are similar to the tenets of the Judaeo-Christian religion. Before delving into Teilhard's theory itself, a few words may be said about the nature of hyperphysics. (A more complete discussion of its nature must, of course, await its elaboration.)

Teilhard admits, from the beginning, that hyperphysics is not physical science in that it encompasses a broader range of phenomena. On the other hand, he believes that eventually physics itself will have to consider this same range of phenomena, implying that hyperphysics is the physics of the future. "The time has come to realize that an interpretation of the universe,—even a positivist one—remains unsatisfying unless it covers the interior as well as the exterior of things; mind as well as matter. The true physics is that which will, one day, achieve the inclusion of man in his wholeness, in a coherent picture of the world."[1]

In THE PHENOMENON OF MAN, Teilhard also states that his work is not metaphysics.[2] As presented, however, this statement is somewhat misleading, for it could be interpreted to mean that, recognizing the nature and value of metaphysics, Teilhard realizes that his phenomenological approach is inherently limited and cannot encroach upon the domain of the metaphysician. A reading of some of the author's correspondence, however, would lead one to believe that Teilhard actually rejects metaphysics, on the grounds that it is rationalistic and static, and he sees his hyperphysics as a replacement for metaphysics.[3] In discussing hyperphysics, therefore, it is important

[1] THE PHENOMENON OF MAN, p. 35.
[2] Ibid., p. 29.
[3] See, for example, Cuénot, op cit., pp. 213 and 233.

to keep in mind that Teilhard himself states that hyperphysics is neither physics nor metaphysics, and more positively, that hyperphysics is an extension of physics and a replacement for metaphysics.

As just stated, Teilhard's rejection of metaphysics is not at all evident in statements such as found in the Preface to THE PHENOMENON OF MAN. His vagueness is understandable, however, in the light of the following facts: This work was completed in 1940, and yet in 1947 permission to publish had not been given, and in that year, Teilhard was ordered by his Superior to write no more philosophy. Regarding this censorship, which was never to be lifted, Teilhard stated in a letter to a friend that he made certain alterations in the text to satisfy the demands of the censor.[1] While, on the one hand, this concern for the censor did not lead Teilhard to alter his thought, it may, on the other hand, have prompted him to omit any direct attacks on metaphysics in the texts which he would have hoped to have had published.

According to Father Elliott, Teilhard's work is philosophical since it seeks to answer the fundamental question: "What is man?" and "What is his future?"[2] This is very true, but it does not mean that hyperphysics, like metaphysics, is a philosophical system, or discipline, completely apart from natural science and hence free from the methods and criteria of science. Hyperphysics, as an extension of physics must, it seems, be in some sense truly scientific. We will consider this point now under the heading "Teilhard's Concept of Truth", and again in the final chapter. We will also consider the relationship between Teilhard's "total world vision" and his world vision as a natural scientist, under the heading "Teilhard's View of the Evolutionary Process".

TEILHARD'S CONCEPT OF TRUTH

Since hyperphysics is based on natural science and is an extension of natural science, it should itself follow the methods of natural science and adhere to the criteria for scientific truth. Consequently, we will preface our discussion of Teilhard's concept of truth with a brief

[1] See, for example, LETTERS FROM A TRAVELLER, p. 310.
[2] F. G. Elliott, 'The World Vision of Teilhard de Chardin', in *International Philosophical Quarterly*, 1, 4, p. 621 (Reprinted in *The Teilhard Review*, Vol. I, Nos. 1 and 2).

account of the scientist's concepts of facts, laws and theories.

Good science begins with facts. Through observation, concepts (or propositions) are arrived at, and these are true concepts inasmuch as they correspond with the facts. A number of related true concepts may, through induction, lead to a more general concept, or a general law. Further observation of these facts could support the law, or could falsify it. Also, general concepts which cannot be tested empirically may arise from the facts and laws; these are known as theories, and they serve to further unify science, explain laws and facts, and lead to new facts. To clarify this and to introduce Teilhard's concept of truth, let us look at the following example.

A physical anthropologist measures certain characteristics of a group of geologically dated primate skulls (e.g. Dryopithecus, Australopithecus, Atlanthropus, Neanderthal, and Homo sapiens; in chronological order). These observations could lead to statements of several facts; for example, the mandibles, as observed in the above-listed order, become progressively smaller. If measurements performed on similar types result in the same conclusions, a general law may be drawn to the effect that more recent primates have smaller mandibles than less recent primates. This law could be further tested simply by measuring more and more mandibles of primate skulls which have been dated. If such experimenting tends to confirm the law, a further generalization which explains this law may be presented: the gradually diminishing mandibles are the result of an evolutionary process through which, because of other related development (of the brain, hands etc.), the heavier mandibles were no longer required for chewing or holding. This general statement cannot be directly empirically tested as can the law, since the evolutionary process is beyond our direct observation. The fundamentalist could counter with the theory that these primates were specially created with successively smaller mandibles, and, at least from the evidence above, one could not prove him wrong.

If one cannot verify or falsify a theory with an empirical test, how then can a theory be evaluated? What are the criteria for a good theory? There are several criteria, but the only one we will mention here is coherence. A good theory should present to us a more coherent picture of the complexity of reality. This, it might be added, is one of the fundamental, if not the fundamental, tasks of science. One of the impelling reasons for accepting the modern theory of evolution as a good theory,—as a theory which seems to closely approximate the truth, is that it not only provides a reasonable explanation for the facts and laws in the example above, but unifies and simplifies a vast array of diverse facts and laws from many different areas of science. It presents a coherent view of what might otherwise appear to be a chaotic universe.

Teilhard himself presents the principle that "the greater coherence is an infallible sign of the greater truth."[1] Elsewhere he states more explicitly that in science the great test of truth is coherence and fecundity. The more order a theory puts into our vision of the world and the more it is capable of directing us towards new knowledge, the more certain a theory is. The true theory is the most advantageous theory.[2]

For Teilhard, therefore, the basic criterion for truth is coherence; not the internal coherence that any good logical system must have, but rather an objective coherence discovered in the universe itself. Not a coherence which is imposed upon the chaotic diversity of reality by the mind, but a coherence which is actually seen to exist in that diversity. This, of course, is not a Teilhardian invention, but a basic principle of all natural science.

The general theory of evolution gives a coherent picture of the universe insofar as it shows the common causes and inter-relationships in the vast diversity of phenomena that exist now and have existed in the past. The theory of evolution also has directed research towards more knowledge, and thus displays the fecundity that Teilhard presents with coherence as his criteria for truth. (It should also be noted that the theory of evolution satisfies other criteria for good theories that Teilhard does not emphasize: it is for example, based on both direct and indirect empirical evidence, and it is compatible with generally accepted facts and other theories.)

The general theory of evolution is, for Teilhard, a starting point—a first principle of his hyperphysics. Evolution, he says is more than a theory: "It is a general condition to which all theories, all hypotheses, all systems must bow and which they must satisfy henceforward if they are to be thinkable and true. Evolution is a light illuminating all facts, a curve that all lines must follow.[3]

[1] THE FUTURE OF MAN, p. 214.
[2] THE VISION OF THE PAST, p. 227.
[3] THE PHENOMENON OF MAN, p. 218.

The view of man within the context of a dynamic, evolving universe is, of course, Teilhard's world vision as a natural scientist. What we have called his total world vision arises from the fact that he sees the whole man within this context. "I repeat that my only aim in these pages—and to this aim all my powers are bent—is to see; that is to say, to develop a homogeneous and coherent perspective of our general extended experience of man. A whole which unfolds."[1]

In dealing with the whole phenomenon of Man, Teilhard is concerned not only with the development of man's material complexity, but also with the development of his interiority, that is to say, the development of consciousness, soul, or spirit. He avoids, as we hope to show, a dualism of matter and spirit; matter and spirit are for Teilhard but two aspects of the one development, aspects which can ultimately be explained by the natural scientist. At the same time, he avoids the type of materialism that would explain consciousness at the higher levels of evolutionary development as nothing more than an advanced manifestation of complexity.

Teilhard's total world vision is then, the view of a continuously developing complexity-consciousness. All developing beings have two aspects: an exteriority or complexity which has been studied by the natural scientists, and an interiority or consciousness which, although considered to some extent by the branches of empirical science that deal with man or even the higher animals, has not been a general object of scientific investigation. Hyperphysics, in dealing with the whole phenomenon, deals with this interior conscious aspect of development, as well as with complexity. It is upon this extended basis, including consciousness, that Teilhard builds his theory of the future of man; a theory of the future of man that shares in the optimism of Christianity rather than the pessimism of a purely mechanistic approach in spite of the fact that it is based on natural science.

TEILHARD'S VIEW OF THE EVOLUTIONARY PROCESS

As we have just seen, the theory of evolution forms the basis of Teilhard's hyperphysics. While Teilhard accepted this theory as presented by modern science, he did have his own interpretation of it—an interpretation which would not necessarily be acceptable to all students of evolution. Evolution, for Teilhard, is a directed development of

[1] *Ibid.*, p. 35.

complexity-consciousness. Inasmuch as orthogenesis is not widely accepted, the notion that evolution is directed would definitely be questioned. Furthermore, the addition of the development of consciousness to the development of complexity may seem tantamount to removing the theory from the realm of the empirical sciences. Since hyperphysics is an extension of physical science this, of course, might be expected; however, it does lead to problems, some of which will be discussed later in this work. At present we will concentrate on the meaning of "a directed development of complexity-consciousness."

Teilhard notes that man at one time was considered to be the centre of a static universe. The fall of the geocentric theory, however, and further scientific development, left man wondering about his place in the universe. In fact, it left him wondering about the place of life itself. Within the newly discovered dimensions of space and time, life is considered to be an accidental occurence of little importance in the overall picture—an epiphenomenon which is born by chance, and will disappear in the same way. The development and decline of the universe can be plotted by the law of increasing entropy as a rising and falling parabola; the history of life on earth, including the history of man, can be represented as a small parabola rising and falling along-side this general parabola of the universe. But such a representation would have little real significance, except to underline man's insignificance.

For Teilhard the truth lies between two extreme views: that man is the centre of the universe, and that man is an insignificant accident in the universe. From the viewpoint of spatial dimensions man certainly is not the centre of the universe, but according to Teilhard, there is another valid point of view. Recent developments in science have laid emphasis on the infinitely large and the infinitely small, and man, existing spatially between two infinities, is relatively insignificant. There is to Teilhard another scale by which to judge the position of man, and that is not the scale of spatial dimensions but the scale of complexity. Besides the infinitely large and infinitely small there is the infinitely complex.[1]

If one abstracts from the spatial dimensions of the universe, and considers it from the point of view of growing complexity, life takes on a new significance. The stars and galaxies, because of their

---

[1] Cf.: THE VISION OF THE PAST, p. 175ff; MAN'S PLACE IN NATURE, p. 17ff; THE FUTURE OF MAN, p. 97ff.

relatively simple composition, are relegated to a lower place on the scale than is the tiny, but very complex, virus. Within this context man takes his place, no longer as the centre of a static world, but as a highly significant element of a world in movement.[1]

In this light, the galaxies, the stars, our own planet, are important, not because of their size, but because they produced the necessary conditions for the emergence of a more complex being. The dimensions of the sun, in themselves, are of little significance from this point of view. What is important is the fact that the sun emits life-sustaining radiation.

At this point we must pay particular attention to Teilhard's definition of the term complexity. By complexity, Teilhard refers not only to the number and variety of the elements forming the ensemble, but also to their arrangement. He states that he strictly confines his use of the word complexity to the meaning of combination, that is "that particular higher form of grouping whose property it is to knit together upon themselves a certain fixed number—whether great or small matters little—of elements, with or without the secondary addition of aggregation or repetition—within a closed whole of determined radius: such as the atom, the molecule, the cell, the metazoon, etc."[2]

Teilhard goes on to emphasize the two-fold characteristic of complexity: a fixed number of elements, and a closed whole, and says that upon this the whole course of his thesis depends.

According to this definition of complexity, a star, though containing more elements than a virus or a man, is less complex. The star is a large, but simple aggregation. It is not a closed whole in that it does not possess an inherent unity, or autonomous activity, as do the virus or the man. The star is a collection of elements which function mainly as independent elements. There are, however, complexities that demonstrate a certain "centricity of action", and an increase in this centricity of action seems to go along with an increase in complexity. In other words, the activities of the elements of some aggregations are decidedly more unified than the activities of elements in others.[3]

[1] Cf.: THE VISION OF THE PAST, p. 216ff.
[2] MAN'S PLACE IN NATURE, p. 20.
[3] The related concepts of complexity and unity are generally used in biology as criteria for development. Cf. for example: George & Muriel Beadle, THE LANGUAGE OF LIFE, Garden City, N.Y., Doubleday, 1966, p. 37. "Higher [with reference to higher animals] means organisms whose increasing complexity of parts is paralleled by the increasing ability of all parts to function together as a unified whole".

And for Teilhard, the term complexity refers to the number and arrangement of elements in these unified or centred aggregations. An increase in complexity is, then, not merely an increase in the number of elements, but also the development of arrangement, and hence an increase in unity and centricity. For example, all of the parts of an automobile disassembled, and piled in a heap, could not act as an automobile, nor would they have the unity required to be called an automobile, simply because, although all the parts are present in the pile, they do not have the arrangement, and are not in the proper combination to be an automobile. A virus is not simply nucleic acid and protein but a specific combination or arrangement of nucleic acid and protein. Furthermore, this specific arrangement no longer acts as nucleic acid and protein separately, but acts as a unit virus.

Teilhard's concept of increasing complexity is in accord with the highly accepted theories of the origin and development of the universe as presented earlier. At the lower levels of development, the degrees of complexity are quite evident: the water molecule is more complex than the hydrogen atom, the protein molecule is more complex than the water molecule. At the more advanced levels of evolution, however, the relative complexities become more obscure. First, there is no single line of evolutionary ascent, but rather, as Teilhard states, a thick column of pluricellular types developing in the general direction of complexity. Secondly, the complexity of the elements on the rays of this column is so great that it would be virtually impossible to compare them in terms of numbers of elements or arrangement. Furthermore, parts of certain beings actually become less complex as the whole develops (for example, the hoof of the horse). It would seem then that since little could be said objectively about the relative complexities of organisms at the more advanced stages of evolutionary development, the concept of complexity would be of little value in attempting to evaluate man's position in the universe. There is, however, according to Teilhard, an empirical criterion for increasing complexity at these levels—a parameter which leads one through the labyrinth of living forms. This criterion of increasing complexity is the development of the nervous system, including the brain; that is, cerebration or cephalization.[1]

Cephalization is considered to be a parameter of com-

[1] Cf.: THE APPEARANCE OF MAN, p. 139; THE PHENOMENON OF MAN, p. 146; MAN'S PLACE IN NATURE, pp. 48, 49.

plexity which is concrete, precise, clear and absolute; therefore it provides a means of plotting the increase in complexity and hence of determining the direction of evolution. According to Teilhard, the result of applying this parameter of cephalization is an axis of development of complexity that runs through the mammals and on to the order Primates and particularly through the family of Anthropoids. This, however, is as far as complexity by itself takes Teilhard. A cephalic index or cranial capacity is not enough in itself to enable one to state that one organism or species or phylum is in a privileged position. As mentioned above, an increased unity of action accompanies increasing complexity, and here we find the additional criterion required.

This unity of action, or centricity, although associated with complexity in some way, is not complexity itself; its introduction leads to new concepts: The cause of action is energy, and a unity of action leads to the idea of some concentration of energy. The activity which gives man his unity as man, and leads him to say that he is "higher" than the other primates is his particular kind of consciousness, that is, self-consciousness. In this way, Teilhard's concept of complexity as a criterion for direction leads to the concepts of energy and consciousness. Consciousness is seen to be an aspect of development which is as fundamental as complexity, and cannot be overlooked in any scientific analysis of the evolutionary process. And it is with the inclusion of consciousness as a parameter of development along with complexity that hyperphysics is born. Evolution is a development of complexity-consciousness. As fundamental as the physicist's laws of entropy or gravitation is the 'Law of complexity-consciousness': 'Left long enough to itself under the prolonged and universal play of chance, matter manifests the property of arranging itself in more and more complex groupings, and at the same time in ever deepening layers of consciousness; this double and combined movement of physical unfolding and psychic interiorisation (or centration) once started, continuing, accelerating and growing to its utmost extent.'[1]

As suggested above, the concepts of consciousness and energy are related in hyperphysics. We will begin our discussion of hyperphysics, therefore, with an analysis of Teilhard's concept of energy.

[1] THE APPEARANCE OF MAN, pp. 139.

CHAPTER TWO

# *Energy in Hyperphysics*

Teilhard was not a physicist, but nevertheless he did have a working knowledge of elementary physics, and used the physicist's concept of energy as the foundation for his own theories on energy and consciousness. A clear understanding of Teilhard's concept of energy requires, therefore, some knowledge of the basic physical concepts. We will begin, consequently, with a short explanation of the physicist's concept of energy to assist those readers who may not know physics.

The concept of energy was arrived at mathematically by means of the space integral of force: $\int$ F.ds (which is called the work). The result is the quantity $\frac{1}{2}$ mv², called the kinetic energy. From the same integral a quantity V was also mathematically deduced—a quantity with the same dimensions as work and kinetic energy, and whose value depends only upon position. V was therefore called energy of position or potential energy.

The instrumentalists (that is, those who believe that the physicist's task is to develop such mathematical formulas and use the ones which seem to work, but it is not his task to explain reality), would be satisfied with an explanation of energy couched in mathematical terms as above. If, on the other hand, these mathematical models do apply to the objective real world, and if the terms such as kinetic energy and potential energy do refer to something that is in that world, then it should be possible to talk about energy as if it exists outside the mathematician's mind as well as in. Furthermore, Teilhard talks about energy that really exists, not about energy as a name given to the result of a mathematical computation. We will, therefore, present an explanation of energy which, while compatible with the mathematical foundations of physics, is not itself mathematical. The physicist should, in general, find it satisfactory. The instrumentalist may object.

## THE PHYSICIST'S CONCEPT OF ENERGY

Energy is defined by the physicist as the capacity to do work. The term 'work' in physics has a very restricted meaning. By definition, work is done when a force is exerted through a distance. If, for example, I push against my desk, and move the desk a certain distance, it could be said that work has been done on the desk. If, on the other hand, I push on the desk, but the desk does not move, no work has been done on the desk, even though force has been exerted. (In mathematical terms, $dW=Fdx$. In the first example, both F, that is, force, and x, that is, distance, have a non-zero value and consequently, there is a value for W. In the second example, F has a certain value, but x is zero—hence no work.) Work is done, therefore, when a force is applied and a certain activity follows. In other words, both the concept of force and activity are involved in the concept 'work'. Energy, therefore, as the capacity to do work, is basically the capacity to perform some activity through the application of some force.

A body has a capacity to do work because of its motion, its position and its internal energy. We will consider each of these separately:

A body has a capacity to do work because of its motion, and energy of motion is called kinetic energy. (Mathematically, kinetic energy equals one-half the mass of the body times the square of the velocity. The mass itself increases with increased velocity, but this relativity effect is negligible except for very high velocity, and so for most purposes the mass may be considered constant.) In physics mass is defined as the quantitative measure of inertia. We know that material bodies resist a change in motion, and the property of bodies which produces this resistance is called inertia. In other words, if a body is moving, a force will be required to change the motion in any way. But if one body exerts a force on another, that other body also exerts an equal but opposite force on the first. Consequently, if force is applied to a body to change its motion, the moving body also exerts a force upon the body which is changing its motion, and in this way the moving body is capable of doing work. The kinetic energy of a body is, therefore, a function of its motion and its inertia.

A body also has a capacity to do work because of its position. Energy of position is called potential energy. A compressed spring or volume of gas has potential energy inasmuch as it will move back to its original position when the compressing force is removed, and in so doing it will gain kinetic energy. A body will also have potential energy because of its position in a gravitational field. Any mass, for example, at rest at the surface of the earth can, because of mutual forces of attraction towards the centre of the earth, fall towards the centre, thus gaining kinetic energy. Similarly an electrically charged body at a point in an electric field, or a magnetized body in a magnetic field, can move in that field because of the forces of attraction or repulsion and thereby attain kinetic energy. Basically then, a body has potential energy because it is in a position to be moved by a force or forces, and hence gain energy of motion, or kinetic energy.

A body has a capacity to do work also because of its internal energy. Internal energy, or energy of composition, arises from the motion and configuration of the particles in a body. A volume of gas at rest will have no external kinetic energy; however, since the individual molecules of the gas in this volume are moving, it has an internal energy of motion. Similarly, if the total volume is electrically neutral, it will have no electrostatic potential energy as a whole, but individual charged molecules within the volume will have electrostatic potential energy.

Internal energy is, then, the kinetic or potential energy of the element within a group of elements, and is therefore not a new kind of energy. Also, potential energy, such as that of a compressed spring or gas, is seen, through analysis, to be a large scale effect of the fundamental potential energies of the elements of the spring, gas, etc. The fundamental potential energies are gravitational, electrostatic and nuclear. Basically then, all energies can be reduced to kinetic and potential energy. Furthermore, kinetic energy and potential energy are not really two different kinds of capacity for work, but, rather, different stages in this capacity. Potential energy is the capacity to obtain kinetic energy which can directly do work because of inertia.


THE CONCEPT OF AVAILABLE ENERGY

According to the first law of thermodynamics, or the law of the conservation of energy, the total amount of energy in the universe remains constant. In other words, energy can be neither created nor annihilated. (In the context of the mass-energy equivalence of relativity physics, the same can be said of mass itself.) The existence of energy, however, does not guarantee that it can always be used to do work. For example, the water surrounding an ocean liner has a large amount of energy, but because of its relatively low temperature it can not be used to power the ocean liner. In fact, not only can the liner not use energy from the water, it will lose energy to the water. This introduces the concept of available energy which will be explained with the aid of the following example:

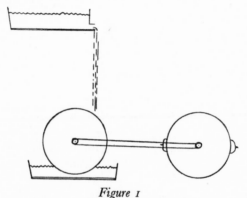

*Figure 1*

*Figure 1* represents a system which is isolated, that is, no mass or energy is transferred to or from the surroundings. It consists of a reservoir of water, a water wheel, and a generator. At the start of the process the water is higher than the wheel, and therefore has available gravitational potential energy to turn the wheel which turns the generator and produces electrical energy. (We have: gravitational potential energy, converted to kinetic energy of the water, converted to kinetic energy of the wheel, converted to kinetic energy of the armature of the generator, converted to electrical potential energy.) When all the water has fallen to the level of the waterwheel a state of equilibrium is reached; and although the water has gravitational potential energy still inasmuch as it could fall further and do work on something that is at a lower level than the waterwheel, there is no more energy available to turn the wheel itself, and thereby produce electrical energy. In the light of this we present the following definition:

available energy is that proportion of energy which could be converted into work by ideal processes which reduce the system to a dead state, that is, a state in equilibrium with its surroundings.

To illustrate a major aspect of available energy, let us add to the above system (*in Figure 1*), in the following diagram:

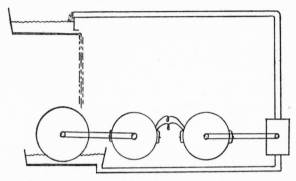

*Figure 2*

In *Figure 2* we have connected an electric motor to the generator and a water pump to the motor in order to pump the water from the level of the wheel back up to the reservoir. In this way we can reverse the process, converting the electrical potential energy produced by the generator into kinetic energy in the motor, transferring this kinetic energy to the pump and then converting the pump's kinetic energy to the water with a final increase in the water's gravitational potential energy, from which the cycle could start again. In this way, the equilibrium or the dead state is avoided by raising the water back to its original height and thereby maintaining its available potential energy. Ideally this system should operate indefinitely. Experience shows, however, that although it will operate longer than the system in *Figure 1*, it will soon reach its own dead state and stop. The reason for this is that some of the energy throughout the process is converted into heat by the friction in the pipes, wheels, wires, etc, and therefore it is not available to do work on the wheel, generator, motor and pump. While some of this heat could be used to do work in the system, some, if not most of it, is no longer available. The work done on the water-wheel will equal the potential energy of the water, less the heat produced and lost. The work done on the generator will equal the kinetic energy of the waterwheel less the heat produced and lost, and so on

c

throughout the process. As a result, water will run out of the reservoir faster than it can be pumped back in, with a consequent decrease in the gravitational potential energy available in the system. Eventually the dead state will be reached as in the first example, when all the water is as low as, or lower than, the waterwheel.

It is clear then that certain conditions must be met before a capacity to do work can actually be used to do work, and therefore there is a distinction between energy and available energy. The law of conservation of energy applies to the fundamental capacity for work itself, and not to the amount of energy which is actually available for work. The second law of thermodynamics, however, is concerned with available energy.

THE SECOND LAW OF THERMODYNAMICS

The example above leads directly to a statement of the second law of thermodynamics: the available energy of an isolated system decreases in all real processes. According to the second law the available energy of the system decreases, and this decrease would be fully accounted for by an increase of non-available energy in the form of heat.

We will now introduce the concept of entropy. Entropy is a thermodynamic property of matter, or more precisely, a function of properties of matter, such as temperature, pressure and volume, which determine the state of the substance. It is an expression of the available energy of a system. Also, since energy is required for arrangement or order, entropy is the measure of the degree of a system's internal order. To be more precise, we should say that entropy is an expression of the lack of available energy of a system and its degree of internal disorder, since an increase in entropy is a decrease in available energy and a consequent decrease in internal order. (The actual physical definition of entropy may be stated as follows: Entropy is the property of matter held constant in a reversible adiabatic process; in mathematical terms: $dS = \dfrac{dQ\,(rev.)}{T}$, where S is entropy, Q is heat, and T, absolute temperature).

As a result of the relationship between entropy and available energy, the second law may be stated in the form of a law of increasing entropy: the entropy of the isolated system increases in all real processes. It also follows that the degree of internal disorder of the isolated system in all real processes increases. (An isolated system refers here, as above, to a system into which or from which no mass or energy is transferred from or to the surroundings.)

According to the theories of the physical universe known to Teilhard, the universe is an isolated system. If this is the case, it would follow from the second law of thermodynamics that the entropy of the universe is increasing and, therefore, its total available energy is decreasing, and, consequently, its internal order is also decreasing. Given the assumption that the second law of thermodynamics will continue to apply to real processes in the future, the universe will eventually reach a state of stable equilibrium in which there will be no available energy, there will be maximum disorder and maximum entropy.

ENTROPY AND THE EVOLUTIONARY PROCESS

In the evolutionary process there is obviously an increase in order or arrangement, and hence a decrease in entropy. According to the second law, such a decrease in entropy cannot exist in an isolated system; the evolving system must receive available energy from outside, that is, from its surroundings. Any increase in order or arrangement requires energy. The individual developing being takes on energy from outside in the form of food, air, energy from the sun, and so on. The whole evolving system on earth (or any planet) is not isolated inasmuch as it derives its energy from the sun (or appropriate star or stars). The evolutionary process is an open system which depends upon available energy from an outside source and, therefore, can increase in order, or decrease in entropy. It can continue to develop, however, only as long as that outside source of energy is available. Assuming that the second law will continue to apply, a time will come when the outside source of energy will not be available and the evolutionary process will come to a halt, and its products will eventually arrive at a state of stable equilibrium with the rest of the system of the universe.

In the context of the second law of thermodynamics, therefore, the development of the whole universe is towards greater entropy or greater disorder. The evolutionary process is looked at as a small open system which can temporarily run against the general flow towards greater entropy by taking on energy from outside. It is, however, no more than a temporary backwash and must eventually succumb to the major current towards increasing entropy.


TEILHARD'S CONCEPT OF ENERGY

As we have seen above, the physicist defines energy as a capacity to do work. Teilhard defines energy as "a capacity for action, or more exactly, for interaction".[1] Teilhard's use of the term action and interaction instead of work makes his definition somewhat broader than that of the physicist. However, his fundamental concept of energy is taken directly from the physical sciences. Since work is defined as force through a distance, the measure of work would also be a measure of action. Even the most complex activity, such as the activity of a human brain, involves forces moving masses through certain distances; however, since these forces and distances are very difficult if not impossible to measure accurately, the physicist's definition of energy as a capacity for work, and work as the product of the applied force and the distance moved, is of no practical value at this level of action. Teilhard is interested primarily in energy as a source of all the actions and interactions which have brought about evolutionary development.

Teilhard regards the evolution of complexity as a continuous development from the simplest forms such as electrons and protons to the most complex of organisms such as man. The continuity of this development is very important and is related directly to Teilhard's principle of coherence. From the point of view of complexity, there are no apparent gaps or jumps in the evolutionary process. The radical difference between life and non-life can be explained in terms of a gradual coming together of macromolecules. The tremendous difference between the higher primates and the lower forms of life may be explained similarly in terms of gradually changing arrangements of elements.

In spite of the fact that radically different beings have been produced by this continuous change in complexity, there is no point at which one must postulate the existence of a radically new kind of energy to account for further transformations. The living organism,

[1] THE PHENOMENON OF MAN, p. 42.

for example, develops in a new way, increasing its complexification from within, but an analysis of the actions and interactions involved in its process of development reveals that they are fundamentally the same as the actions and interactions of the non-living world and flow from the same kind of energy. "In last analysis" states Teilhard, "somehow or other there must be a single energy operating in the world."[1]

Teilhard does not say that there must be a single energy operating in the physical world; simply that there must be a single energy operating in the world. In other words, the energy that produces the attraction between the electron and proton in the hydrogen atom is the same kind of energy that produces the most profound and sophisticated actions in man, such as thinking and willing. This position may be interpreted as a purely materialistic one: the higher activities of man can be seen through analysis to be no more than complex kinds of physical activity. From this point of view we could say that the one energy operating in the world is physical energy. Teilhard insists, however, that the physicist has looked at the world only from the outside, has looked only at the without of things; in other words, he has studied reality from the point of view of its complexity, and even much of his knowledge of energy is in terms of complexity. Hence the materialistic position, just stated, could be interpreted to mean that the higher activities of man, such as thinking and willing, are no more than manifestations of a high degree of complexity. As Lord Russell puts it, man is nothing more than an accidental collocation of atoms.

The path that Teilhard follows from his postulate of one energy in the world is, however, somewhat different from that of the materialist. Teilhard does not analyse man into his simplest components and then explain man in terms of these components. Man is indeed a collocation of atoms, but, since we know more about man than about the atom, should not our explanation of man begin at the level of man, rather than at the level of the atom? Furthermore, could not an explanation of lower forms also begin at the level of man? Rather than starting with the atom and working up to man, Teilhard begins with what he knows of man's activities and, under the assumption of a continuous development, proceeds "downwards" towards the atom.

Man is certainly aware of his own complexity, but he is also

[1] *Ibid.*, p. 63.

aware of some activities such as consciousness and willing which could be classified as psychic activities. Moreover, he knows of analogous activities in other organisms. Furthermore, where psychic activities are found, they are seen to be essential for the development of the beings in which they are found. The individual and the species develop because of an awareness of the environment, and affinities for those things which aid development. An animal, for example, is aware of food, and, without knowing food as good, as in the case of the self-conscious animal, has an affinity, or an inclination for this food.

This much is quite certain: We know that truly human activity is based on consciousness, and is by definition therefore, psychic. Some animal activities, at least those of the higher animals, are similar enough to man's psychic activities for us to be sure that they also flow from consciousness and, therefore, are also psychic. Below the level of the animal, however, psychic activity is not evident. The activity of a plant, for instance, is not similar to human activity, and so consciousness is not apparent. A study of plant life would not necessarily lead one to postulate the existence of psychic activity at this level. If it is known, however, that the vegetable kindgom and the animal kingdom are but two segments of a continuous spectrum of living things, and that the development from plant life to animal life was a continuous process, then one could conclude that the activities of plants and animals should arise from a similar kind of energy. (There are, in fact, life-forms such as euglena which cannot be classified as either animal or vegetable, and are seen as lying on the border between the two kingdoms.) There is, at least, no evidence of a new kind of energy at work at any point of the evolutionary process. With this in mind, we may look more closely at the activities of vegetative life to see what analogies to animal life can be discovered.

The plant, like the animal, requires certain things for its proper development: sunlight, water, minerals etc. And, like the animal, the plant acts to get these things. The leaves, for example, will turn towards the sun, and the roots grow towards a source of moisture. There is, then, evidence of an openness of the plant to its environment, and an affinity to those things which aid development. This openness to reality, and the corresponding affinities, are more simple and primitive than those activities which we normally call psychic in animals and men, but in view of the continuity of development spoken of above, they are not essentially different kinds of activities, but, rather different degrees of the same activities. For this reason Teilhard refers to these activities also as psychic, and to the openness to reality as consciousness, a word which he uses in a very wide sense, denoting any kind of psychism.[1] The fundamental activities of all living things are, therefore, psychic activities.

Within the context of evolution, life itself is seen to be a continuous development from non-life. Again, therefore, there is no reason to suppose the existence of an essentially different kind of activity in non-living forms, and there is evidence of activity which is analogous to the activity of living things. At the threshold of life itself the activity of the complex molecules cannot be considered blind or accidental. For example, in cell division, the neucleotide bases of nucleic acid almost always pair in the same way (adenine with thymine, cytosine with guanine). In the exceptional case of a mutation, the change in pairing is due not to blind chance, but to a shifting in the hydrogen bond, and as such is predictable. There is a definite affinity between certain sets of molecules which in itself indicates an openness to their surroundings; and the fact that the molecule is a part of a continuous spectrum of beings, some of which definitely are conscious, further confirms the existence of some sort of rudimentary consciousness at the molecular level.

The analogy may be extended more deeply into the realm of non-living things. For example, the activities of particles in fields would indicate an openness of the particle to its environment, and a consequent affinity. An electron will move one way in a positive electrostatic field, another way in a negative field. It will react in one way to a charged body, and in another way to an uncharged body. These activities are not blind or purely accidental. They could not be explained on the assumption that the particles are completely closed off from their environment. (To say that the particle is "pulled" or "pushed" by the field merely temporarily shifts our attention to the particle which is the source of the field. If a proton "pushes" another proton, and "pulls" an electron, it must, in some way, distinguish between protons and electrons.)

To say that this openness to reality which the fundamental particles (and all inanimate particles) possess is consciousness seems at first a most unwarranted and ludicrous statement. Even the application of the term to vegetative life appears to be out of the ordinary, and

[1] Cf. THE PHENOMENON OF MAN, p. 57.

to use it at the elementary levels of pre-life seems to be stretching the analogy much too far. Looking back through the continuous spectrum of evolution, however, where does the analogy cease? Is not consciousness, as we know it, a highly developed openness to reality? And therefore, could not the simple openness of the atom and the molecule be just the most rudimentary form of consciousness? Teilhard's answer to these questions is quite clear. "The within, consciousness, and then spontaneity—three expressions for the same thing. It is no more legitimate for us experimentally to fix an absolute beginning to these three expressions of one and the same thing than to any other lines of the universe".[1]

Consciousness, for Teilhard, has no beginning in the evolutionary process, but is co-extensive with complexity. With regard to the affinities which are the psychic activities following from consciousness, Teilhard says: "Considered in its full biological reality, love—that is to say the affinity of being with being—is not peculiar to man . . . By rights, to be certain of its presence in ourselves, we should assume its presence, at least in an inchoate form, in everything that is."[2]

Whether we call them consciousness, awareness, or simply openness to reality—love or affinity, these psychic activities exist at all levels of development, from the sub-atomic particles to man. Furthermore, these are the activities that produce development at every level; there is no activity which is not fundamentally psychic.

If all activity is psychic and there is one energy as the source of all activity, it would follow that this one energy should be called psychic energy, and this in fact is exactly what Teilhard says: "All energy is psychic in nature."[3]

Once again we should state that the essential point being made is that there is only one kind of energy operating in the universe. Since the highest manifestations of this energy have been called psychic, Teilhard sees fit to call all energy psychic. This is not so much a radical departure from the materialist view looked at above, but rather a shift in emphasis and a different point of view which opens the door for the development of hyperphysics. The materialistic or positivistic point of view places emphasis on analysis, and the explanation of higher organisms in terms of physical phenomena and laws. Consequently,

---

[1] THE PHENOMENON OF MAN, p. 57.
[2] Ibid., p. 264.
[3] Ibid., p. 64. (In the first editions psychic was misprinted as physical.)

because of the physicist's concern for complexity, a mechanistic explanation results. Teilhard, on the other hand, rather than attempting to explain the higher in terms of the lower, uses what is evident in the activities of higher organisms to shed light on the activities of the lower levels of development, thereby placing the emphasis on psychic activities.

It should be noted that Teilhard is not replacing "physical activity" with "psychic activity", nor "physical energy" with "psychic energy". Nor is he adding some mysterious entity in order to explain activity. What he is doing, basically, is emphasizing the unity, continuity, and homogeneity of the whole evolutionary process, by stressing the position that there is one kind of activity, and therefore one kind of energy throughout this process. The activities seen by the physicist or the chemist are fundamentally the same as the activities seen by the psychologist, or any human being through introspection. Whereas some would say that man operates on the same kind of energy as the atom, that is, physical energy, Teilhard prefers to say that the atom operates on the same kind of energy as man, that is, psychic energy. Furthermore, in discussing psychic activity at the human level, we normally go beyond the complexity of the organism, and speak of another aspect of matter which we call consciousness, or mind, or even spirit. Teilhard's approach to the problem of activity and energy postulates the existence of this other aspect of matter at every level of evolutionary development. The two faces of matter are, for Teilhard, complexity and consciousness, or a without and a within. The within is coextensive with the without, that is, some form of consciousness, or openness to reality, exists at every level. Evolution is, therefore, seen to be a development of complexity-consciousness.

No dualism is intended here; at least no dualism in the Cartesian sense, or as found in some scholastic philosophers who would seem to distinguish between body and soul as between separate entities. Complexity and consciousness are presented by Teilhard simply as distinct aspects of every material being. Consciousness requires a certain degree of complexity, and the maintenance and development of complexity requires consciousness. The two are intimately interconnected in every being, and yet cannot be identified with each other.

Since the statement that all energy is psychic is not the postulation of a new kind of energy, but simply a different way of looking at physical energy, and furthermore, since he wishes to base his hyperphysics on physics, Teilhard is bound to adhere to the laws of physics concerning energy. One of these laws which Teilhard accepts, that is, the second law of thermodynamics, presents him with a major problem in his syntheses; such a major problem, in fact, that the whole of his hyperphysical theory revolves around the solution of it. According to Bernard Towers: "The fundamental pioneering achievement of Teilhard was to make sense out of the two most famous, but apparently contradictory, scientific ideas to come out of the nineteenth century: the theory of biological evolution on the one hand, and the second law of thermodynamics on the other."[1]

As we have seen above, according to the second law of thermodynamics, or the law of increasing entropy, the total amount of available energy in the universe is diminishing. Therefore at some point in the future, there will be no more energy available for the maintenance and development of complexity; the process of evolutionary development will reverse and run down to a state of complete disorder or, in the physicist's terms, 'a state of maximum entropy'. It would seem then, that the forecast of an ultimate destiny for man, in a perfected state, would have to be based on data which lies outside the field of the natural sciences.[2] Teilhard, however, presents a theory of energy which leads to this forecast within the context of hyperphysics and at the same time respects the laws of thermodynamics.

To his assumption that all energy is psychic, Teilhard adds, "that in each particular element this fundamental energy is divided in two distinct components: a tangential energy which links the element with all others of the same order (that is to say of the same complexity and the same centricity) as itself in the universe; and a radial energy which draws it towards ever greater complexity and centricity—in other words forwards."[3]

---

[1] *The Teilhard Review*, Vol. 1, No. 2, p. 52.
[2] This of course would not be the case if either the law of entropy or the prediction based upon it were found to be invalid, and it should be noted that some scientists today feel that this may be the case. Both the law and the prediction based upon it, however, are widely accepted in the scientific community, and furthermore, Teilhard seemed to accept them without hesitation. As a result, his hyperphysical theory is based on the assumption that the law is valid, and hence, for the purposes of this exposition, it will be considered to be valid. Since the second law of thermodynamics presents a problem in Teilhard's hyperphysics, the rejection of this law should do nothing but strengthen his theory. For a discussion of the rejection of the law of increasing entropy, see: E. Schatzman, THE ORIGIN AND EVOLUTION OF THE UNIVERSE, London, 1966, Appendix 2.
[3] THE PHENOMENON OF MAN, p. 64, The French 'se divise' might better be translated as 'divides itself' rather than 'is divided'.

Unfortunately, and in spite of the importance of this particular point, Teilhard does not give a detailed and explicit explanation of these two components of energy. In the following discussion, therefore, we may at time go beyond the actual words of Teilhard on this matter; however, it is hoped that what will be said will remain Teilhardian.

The division of the fundamental psychic energy into two components follows directly from Teilhard's position that evolution is a development of complexity—consciousness. He says that, "there exist in every corpuscle two levels of operation: one (let us call it tangential) binding physico-chemically, that is to say by way of complexity, the corpuscle in question to all other corpuscles in the universe: the other (let us call it radial or axial) leading directly from consciousness to consciousness, and manifesting itself, on the level of humanity, in the different psychological phenomena . . . of unanimity and co-reflexion."[1]

The latter level of operation, that is, the radial, is the more fundamental of the two, and its source of operation is called radial energy. The "binding operation" on the other level is actually the operation of producing new arrangements, and this is brought about, not by a different kind of energy, but by an aspect of the one fundamental energy, which Teilhard called tangential energy.

There may be some objection to this interpretation of Teilhard's concept of energy for he does, at times, seem to imply that radial and tangential energies are two distinct kinds of energy (see, for example, the footnote following the above quotation). He states clearly, nevertheless, that there is only one energy, and that radial and tangential energies are components of the one energy.

Teilhard further identifies radial energy with psychic energy, and tangential energy with physical energy, which seems to conflict with the statement that all energy is psychic. The explanation for this may be found in the fact that the two levels of operation are traditionally known as physical and psychic. The fundamental capacity for any activity, according to Teilhard, is psychic. Activities which flow from this psychic energy are traditionally divided into psychic and physical, and energy as the source of the former is called radial, while energy as the source of the latter is called tangential.

In the language of the physicist, radial acceleration is an

[1] THE APPEARANCE OF MAN, p. 265.

acceleration towards the centre, radial force is a force towards the centre; in other words, the term radial in this context means "towards the centre". The term tangential, when referring to velocity or acceleration in physics, means along the tangent, and away from the centre. This appears to be Teilhard's reason for using these terms, for he points out that strongly centred particles have a high degree of radial energy, whereas particles with less centreity have less radial but more tangential energy. Increased centriety or increased concentration of the source of psychic activity is found in beings higher up the scale of natural development, and so, as beings become more and more centred, or more and more highly developed, the tangential energy becomes less evident and the radial energy become more evident.

As a further clue to the meaning of radial energy, Teilhard identifies it, in THE PHENOMENON OF MAN, with love. Love, he states, does not exist only on the human level. In fact, in order for it to exist in man, it must exist at all levels of development. Teilhard defines love simply as the affinity of being with being. He equates it with radial energy when he states that driven by the forces of love, the fragments of the world seek each other, so that the world may come into being (which statement, he insists, is neither metaphor nor poetry).[1] This identification is made quite definite, in a more explicit way, in the following: "Only union through love and in love (using the word 'love' in its widest and most real sense of 'mutual internal affinity'), because it brings individuals together, not superficially and tangentially but centre to centre, can physically possess the property of not merely differentiating but personalizing the elements which comprise it."[2]

This identification is a consequence of and further evidence of Teilhard's principle of coherence and his belief in the unity of structure and mechanism in reality. He recognizes that the analogy between human love and the affinities of lower beings is quite obscure. But whether the relationship can be seen or not, he insists that all affinities are fundamentally the same. Furthermore, it is love energy, or radial energy, that produces development at all levels.

The concept that love exists at all levels of material beings, and all affinities are fundamentally the same, is certainly not a part of modern science. Even the term "attraction" would be used by the

[1] THE PHENOMENON OF MAN, p. 264.
[2] THE FUTURE OF MAN, p. 235.

scientist without reference to the attractions associated with human love. This concept, nevertheless, is an essential part of Teilhard's hyperphysics.

We will continue this interpretation of Teilhard's concept of energy by comparing it with the physicist's idea of energy. But before going on to that some reflection upon the basic notions just presented may be helpful.

We see Teilhard's principle of coherence at work in his insistence that, "somehow or other, there must be a single energy operating in the world".[1] This does not, however, lead to a materialistic monism or positivistic position of the kind that would reduce everything to more or less complex arrangements of atoms, and explain all activity in terms of the fundamental packets of energy. On the contrary, Teilhard elevates matter by explaining the lower in terms of the higher—by arguing, in effect, that if we know that there is psychic energy, and if we accept the hypothesis that there is only one energy, then we also must accept the hypothesis that all energy is psychic.

This gives Teilhard a coherent foundation for hyperphysics, and guards against dualism which he rejects as unscientific. It also leaves him with somewhat of a dilemma, for he sees two rather different types of activity in the evolutionary process. There is the tendency towards development itself, which is the fundamental activity, and there is the activity of forming new arrangements which is absolutely necessary for the development of complexity-consciousness. Psychic energy must divide itself, then, into two components which are the source of these two types of activity: radial energy—the source of the fundamental movement towards greater complexity-consciousness; and tangential energy—the source of the required arrangements.

We will proceed now to a further analysis of this theory in the light of what the scientist says about energy.

THE RELATIONSHIP BETWEEN TEILHARD'S CONCEPT OF ENERGY AND THAT OF MODERN SCIENCE

Since Teilhard's hyperphysics is based on modern science, we would expect that not only should his concept of energy be compatible with that of modern science, but also that it should be based upon the

[1] THE PHENOMENON OF MAN, p. 63.

scientist's concept of energy. Teilhard was not a physicist; he was a palaeontologist, and consequently, the emphasis in his work is upon the higher levels of evolutionary development rather than on the problem of energy itself. As a result, the very important and fundamental discussion of energy in Teilhard is rather vague, and the actual relationships between his basic psychic energy and its two components (that is, radial and tangential energy), with the physicist's concept of energy is not too clear. We will now attempt to make a more explicit connection between Teilhard's concept of energy and that of modern physics. Since much of what follows was not stated by Teilhard, we can present it only as a suggested interpretation of his concept of energy and argue in favour of its validity by showing that it is compatible with what he has actually said, and with modern concepts of energy.

As we stated above, the several energies spoken of by the physicist, such as potential energy, kinetic energy, and internal energy, are not really different kinds of energy, but rather different stages in the fundamental capacity for work. Internal energy is the kinetic or potential energy of elements within a group of elements, and potential energy is the capacity to attain kinetic energy which can directly do work because of inertia. A body can do work because it is in motion, or has kinetic energy, and it has kinetic energy because it had a certain potential energy. We may ask then, why does a body have potential energy? The physicist may answer that a body has potential energy because of its position in a field and may refer to the forces of attraction or repulsion that exist because of the field; however, the physicist will not say anything about the fundamental nature of this potential energy, or of these forces. As Teilhard puts it, the physicist is still concerned primarily with the without of things. Hyperphysics on the other hand, attempting to go one step further than physics to the within of things, would be more interested in the nature of potential energy.

Teilhard's assumption that all energy is psychic is concerned with the nature of energy itself. It identifies energy, as the source of psychic activity, with consciousness and the affinities or tendencies ('love') which follow from consciousness. We could not say that this is an ultimate explanation of the nature of energy for, indeed, we know very little about consciousness even at the human level of development. Nevertheless (whether right or wrong), it is a more ultimate explanation of energy than the definitions in terms of space integrals of force, or the definition of energy as a capacity for work. Let us consider the assumption that energy is psychic as applied to what would ordinarily be thought of as purely physical phenomena.

Water falling from a certain height will turn a waterwheel. Work is done on the wheel because the falling water has kinetic energy. The water has this kinetic energy because of its position above the waterwheel, that it, because of its potential energy. In other words, since the water is higher than the wheel, it can fall on the wheel, and it falls because of gravitational attraction. For Teilhard, this attraction would be explained in terms of an awareness of water for other material bodies, in this case, the earth, and following this awareness, a fundamental affinity between the water as a material body, and the earth as another material body; and this awareness and affinity of being for being is psychic energy. Thus the potential energy of the water is a result of its awareness of, and affinity for, other material bodies; that is, it is a result of its psychic energy.

It may seem unnecessary to introduce terms such as psychic, affinity and awareness in this case instead of using the physicist's concepts of field or gravitational attraction. The introduction of these terms is not superfluous, however, for it does say something about the nature of this activity by drawing an analogy between it and activities at other levels of development. (This point will be discussed at greater length later.)

Let us now consider some of the things that Teilhard says about radial or psychic energy to see if they confirm the above thesis: that is, that radial energy is the basis of potential energy and hence of kinetic energy as well.

Teilhard states that radial energy draws the element towards ever greater complexity or centricity, and this statement seems compatible with our position. The electron and proton, for example, are drawn towards a greater complexity in the formation of an atom, and this is accomplished by the electrostatic attraction between the electron and proton, which, in Teilhardian terms, would be described as a mutual awareness and affinity between these particles. The atom, with greater complexity and centricity than its component sub-atomic particles, also has a higher degree of radial energy which draws it further towards union with other atoms to form more complex units, such as heavier atoms or molecules.

Teilhard also states that radial energy leads directly from consciousness to consciousness, manifesting itself on the human level in the different psychological phenomena such as unanimity and co-reflection.[1] This statement also relates radial energy with the fundamental psychic activities of consciousness and affinity.

Teilhard says further that radial energy escapes from entropy. ⌠This point will be discussed at greater length later, and we will simply note here that the law of entropy does not apply *directly* to the fundamental energies such as electrostatic energy, nuclear energy or gravitational energy, and therefore, does not apply to the source of these energies.⌡(The question which arises here is: if it is simply a case of entropy not applying to radial energy, why does Teilhard say that radial energy escapes from entropy? This question will also be discussed later.)

Teilhard states that radial energy increases with the arrangement of the tangential. As we have already said, the more complex structures have higher degrees of consciousness and greater affinities, and hence could be said to have a higher degree of radial energy.

We will now go on to Teilhard's concept of tangential energy, which seems to be even less clear than his concept of radial energy. Before presenting our theory of the possible relationship between tangential energy and the physicist's concept of energy, we must introduce a couple of concepts from thermodynamics.

Both the Gibbs and Helmholtz functions are functions of a body's temperature, entropy and internal energy. The decreases in each of these functions equals the maximum energy that can be freed by the body and made available for work. Therefore these functions are called free energy. Free energy, consequently, refers to thermodynamic potential, which is the energy required to bring a unit mass of a substance from an arbitrarily defined initial state to any other state. In other words, free energy is the total amount of energy available to bring about a particular arrangement. An analysis of Teilhard's concept of tangential energy would indicate that tangential energy is free energy as defined by the Gibbs or Helmholtz functions.

First it should be noted that free energy is not a different kind of energy, but rather a particular aspect of energy. Free energy is simply energy which is available for transformations or new arrange-

---

[1] THE APPEARANCE OF MAN, p. 265; and for a further explanation of these terms, *ibid.*, p. 252ff.

ments. Similarly for Teilhard, since he states that there is only one kind of energy, tangential energy is a particular aspect of the fundamental psychic energy, and furthermore, he states that it is that aspect of energy which links elements with those of the same order. In other words, and he states this explicitly, it is energy of arrangement, and on occasion he uses the term free tangential energy.[1]   — *form ∴ information?*

According to the science of thermodynamics, the total amount of free available energy in the universe is diminishing; however, a more complex body has a greater amount of free energy than a simpler body. Similarly for Teilhard, tangential energy of arrangement obeys the laws of thermodynamics, particularly the law of increasing entropy, but increases at higher levels of complexity.[2] With regard to the relationship between tangential energy and radial energy, Teilhard says that new arrangements are prompted by radial energy, but that radial energy and tangential energy are not directly transformable, but are interdependent. Although a bit vague, these statements do seem to be basically compatible with our suggested interpretation. It is obviously not because energy is available that a transformation comes about, but because energy is the fundamental capacity to do work. In Teilhardian terms, it is the radial component of energy that actually brings about the transformation. As we have seen in our general discussion of energy and entropy, however, not all energy can be made available to do work at all times, hence, radial and tangential energy are not directly transformable.

Teilhard refers to tangential energy as physical energy and radial energy as psychic energy, and also states that the physicist is interested primarily in the former. This statement is also compatible with the thesis we have presented. Radial energy refers to the fundamental nature of energy in which the natural scientist has not been interested, whereas tangential energy refers to energy as available to do work, and furthermore refers to a measurable aspect of energy, and therefore to an aspect of energy which directly concerns the physicist.

(The physicist, of course, is interested in all aspects of energy, including aspects not directly related to energy as available. Teilhard makes a further distinction, which, although it doesn't appear to play an important role in his synthesis, does possibly leave room for energy

[1] Cf. THE PHENOMENON OF MAN, p. 65.
[2] See, for example, THE APPEARANCE OF MAN, p. 265, and THE PHENOMENON OF MAN, p. 65.

D

as physical and measurable, but not directly related to free energy. He states in a footnote in THE PHENOMENON OF MAN that possibly tangential energy should be divided into the tangential energy of arrangement, of which we have already spoken, which he says exists to a greater degree at higher levels of development, and a tangential energy of radiation which, he says, is more apparent at lower levels.[1] Radiation refers to the emission and propagation of energy through space or through a material medium in the form of waves. The term can refer to any type of wave propagation, but usually, when left unspecified, refers to electromagnetic waves. Radiation, therefore, is a very important aspect of physical energy and Teilhard in discussing the early evolution of the universe does himself refer to radiant energy.[2] Teilhard, being interested primarily in the evolutionary process itself, would be mainly concerned with energy of arrangement; however, in presenting a rather fundamental discussion of energy it would be inappropriate to imply that the only energy of interest to the physicist is energy of arrangement. Hence, possibly—the reason for this further distinction. It should be noted as well that electromagnetic radiation is actually propagated at the atomic or sub-atomic levels, but exists, of course, in all complex bodies inasmuch as all complex bodies are composed of sub-atomic particles. It should also be noted that free energy exists at every level of complexity, but is greater at the higher levels.)

Briefly summarizing the suggested relationship between Teilhard's concept of energy and the physicist's concept of energy, we may say the following: There is first of all, according to Teilhard, only one fundamental kind of energy in the universe; this energy is psychic energy, and the term radial energy refers to energy from this particular point of view. Psychic energy would then be the fundamental source of the energies discussed by the physicist. Psychic energy would be the source of potential energy, which is in turn the source of kinetic energy. The physicist, as a physicist, is not directly concerned with the fundamental nature of energy, and therefore is not concerned with psychic energy or radial energy as such.[3]

[1] THE PHENOMENON OF MAN, p. 65.
[2] See, for example, THE APPEARANCE OF MAN, p. 211ff.
[3] With regard to the idea that there is only one fundamental energy it could be noted that recent experiments at Princeton University lead to the conclusion that gravitational effects, like electromagnetic ones, are due to the interaction of matter with one or more of three kinds of classical field, which possibly is a single tensor field. Cf. Dicke, Roll and Weber, "Gravity Experiments" in MODERN SCIENCE AND TECHNOLOGY, Princeton, N.J., Van Nostrand, 1965, p.1ff.

The statement that psychic energy is the source of potential energy should be further clarified. Potential energy is energy of position, but obviously position itself could not be the cause of energy. We are saying that a body in a certain position has energy, that is, can do work, because of its awareness (consciousness) of and affinity for other bodies. As we have seen above, the physicist measures this energy with reference to the position of the body in a field. We might say, then, that from the point of view of measurement, potential energy is energy of position; from the point of view of its nature, potential energy is psychic energy. Furthermore, the measurement of the amount of energy of position indicates the amount of kinetic energy a body can acquire. The statement that the fundamental energy is psychic tells us why the body acquires this kinetic energy.

Teilhard, then, distinguishes between psychic energy as the fundamental source of all energy and tangential energy as the aspect of energy considered by the physicist. The most important physical aspect of energy, at least from the point of view of the theory of evolution, is energy of arrangement, or free energy as defined by the Gibbs and Helmholtz functions. And this is what is referred to by Teilhard when he speaks of tangential energy of arrangement.

May we repeat that this interpretation of Teilhard's concept of energy is presented as a theory, and one of the major objections to this particular interpretation is: If this is what Teilhard meant, why didn't he state it explicitly? Why for example, did not Teilhard simply use the term free energy rather than tangential energy of arrangement or free tangential energy? First, it might be pointed out that since Teilhard's treatment of energy is not too explicit, any detailed interpretation of it could be met with exactly the same objection. It could also be pointed out that since Teilhard was not himself a physicist, nor were his readers to be physicists, he may have quite naturally stayed away from any detailed or explicit use of terminology from the physical sciences. Since, however, Teilhard was a scientist, and wished to base his hyperphysics on science, it is reasonable to assume that, wherever possible and to the greatest extent possible, he would wish to use the accepted results of physical science. The very fact that compatibility has been demonstrated between Teilhard's words and scientific theory goes a long way towards justifying this interpretation.

Another problem in attributing the above interpretation to Teilhard is that he refers to the two energies as components of the one fundamental energy, and speaks of their mutual independence which, he says, is as clear as their interrelation when we try to couple the two of them together. As we have already stated, potential energy cannot always be completely transformed into available energy, however, since available energy is just potential energy in a particular context or position it would seem impossible to speak of the mutual independence of the two. Statements such as these increase the possibility that Teilhard himself had not intended the interpretation of his two energies that has been presented above. We still feel however, that this interpretation is Teilhardian in spirit for it maintains the scientific basis which he wanted for his hyperphysics. As we shall see, it enables hyperphysics to develop as Teilhard intended it; it answers some of the questions which Teilhard himself raised, and it avoids the dualism which Teilhard wished to avoid, but nevertheless, he came very close to not avoiding in statements such as the above, referring to the independence of the two energies.

In the light of our interpretation of the relationship between Teilhard's concept of energy and that of the physicist we will now go on to discuss the relationship between tangential energy and radial energy, between the without and the within. The nature of this relationship, of course, depends upon the nature of the two energies themselves, and consequently the vagueness of Teilhard's treatment of the two energies is carried on into his treatment of the relationship between them.

The within and the without, states Teilhard, "are constantly associated and in some way pass into each other. But it seems impossible to establish a simple correspondence between their curves."[1] He states this because of the quantitative disproportion that he sees between the two energies. For example, the highest human activities of thinking and willing may be performed with an almost negligible amount of physical (i.e. tangential) energy. (Experiments using an electroencephalogram to measure brain waves have shown that, whereas the physical activity of the brain of a human subject performing very simple mental tasks is easily measurable, the physical activity of the brain of a subject who is solving very difficult mathematical problems is not detectable. In other words, the physical activity of the brain appears to decrease as the mental activity increases. Other experiments indicate that the amplitude of brain waves

[1] THE PHENOMENON OF MAN, p. 64.

does not continue to increase as mental development increases over a human subject's lifetime but in fact levels off to a constant value at the time when the subject's mental capacities begin to flourish.

These experiments just referred to would not be known by Teilhard; however, they do help to confirm his position with regard to the disproportion between physical and mental energy). He concludes from this disproportion that between the within and without of things the interdependence of energy is incontestable, but that there is no hope of discovering a mechanical equivalent for will or thought. In other words, he insists that the higher forms of mental activity cannot be attributed to complexity or arrangement. How then is the interdependence of energy between the within and without of things to be explained?

We must first try to add some precision to the definitions of the within and the without of things. Teilhard identifies the within with consciousness and spontaneity, and hence the within is "the psychic force" of matter,[1] and, in the light of our interpretation as well as Teilhard's own statement that there is just one fundamental energy, the within would be the source of all energy. The without of things, which according to Teilhard has been the object of scientific investigation and also the only part of reality seen in a mechanistic approach, could be identified with complexity or arrangement. Just as radial or psychic energy is related to the within of things, Teilhard relates tangential energy to the without. Whereas the within, may be considered to be the source of radial energy, the without could not be considered to be the source of tangential energy. Complexity and arrangement cannot be a source of energy since they themselves are produced by energy; and therefore we may say that the without of things is brought about by tangential energy. This statement is certainly in line with the physicist's view of free energy of arrangement, and also with Teilhard's view that there is just one fundamental energy and therefore, as it should follow, there is just one fundamental source of all energy, that is, the within or psychic energy itself.

Each material being has, then, two "faces" or aspects: an aspect of complexity which Teilhard calls the without, and a psychic aspect called the within. The within is the consciousness or fundamental energy of the being. This psychic energy is centred or concentrated as complexity increases so that, although each of the component parts of

---

[1] *Ibid.*, p. 72.

a complex being has its own energy, the being as a whole also has its own energy which is, apparently, not simply the sum of the energy of the parts. For example, the atoms of iron and oxygen and hydrogen in a human body each have a particular openness to their environment and certain affinities whereby they act in specific ways; but also, the whole man, as a unified organism, has a consciousness and affinities whereby he acts as a man, and develops as a man. Human activity is brought about, not by the sum total of the activities of the parts, but by a concentration of psychic energy, a psychic centre or a human within.

Using Teilhard's analysis of the two energies, and the interpretation in terms of physical science as presented above, we will now give some explanation of their interrelationships.

Every material body has a capacity for action or work. The physicist refers to this capacity as the body's potential energy. Teilhard sees it as a consciousness of the environment followed by affinities for certain other bodies in that environment, and refers to it as psychic energy. Under the proper conditions, a body with this psychic energy can act with another such body to produce a new arrangement. This new arrangement, with its increased complexity, would have, according to the physicist, a somewhat different potential energy than its components and, according to Teilhard, a higher degree of awareness for its environment, and the possibility of new affinities. It could, therefore, interact with other bodies to form further arrangements with still greater complexity. To further clarify this explanation we may use the following example:

An electron is a negatively charged sub-atomic particle, and a proton a positively charged sub-atomic particle. Since unlike charges attract, electrons and protons attract each other and given the proper conditions, there is the chance that the electron and proton will interact to form a hydrogen atom. The physicist would say that when the electron is in the field, or area of influence of the proton (or vice versa), the electron has a certain amount of electrical potential energy. It can, therefore, move towards the proton and the above mentioned interaction could take place. It is interesting to note here that the potential energy of the electron is not known or measured directly, but by the motion of the electron. In other words, the potential energy that the electron has at a point A with respect to another point B is equal to the energy that would be required to move the electron from the point B to the point A. It is clear from this that the physicist's concept of potential energy is defined in terms of the movement of the mass in question, and says nothing about the nature of the potential energy. On the other hand, Teilhard would say that the electron has a certain awareness of its environment and in this particular case, an awareness of the proton (this Teilhardian concept corresponds to the physicist's concept of field) and that the electron has a subsequent affinity for protons (and vice versa). The electron and proton, therefore, move together and the interaction is made possible, given the right conditions. The hydrogen atom which is produced is more complex than either the electron or proton, and it does have new affinities. For example, the hydrogen atom may attract and be attracted by an oxygen atom, and under the right conditions, two hydrogen atoms and one oxygen atom may combine to form a still greater complexity— the water molecule.

Similar examples could be found higher up the evolutionary scale, both in the transformations which occur in the production of more complex beings from simpler beings, and in the different arrangements which are required in the development of an individual organism. The search for and acquisition of food by an animal, for example, could be explained in terms of an interplay of psychic activities (that is, consciousness, and appetite), and physical activities at the cellular, molecular and atomic levels. Such explanations would appear to be infinitely more complex than the simple example used above, nevertheless, the nature of the interdependence of the psychic and the physical, that is, the within and the without, would be, according to Teilhard, fundamentally the same. Similarly, any human activity would involve an interrelationship of the psychic activities of consciousness and willing on the one hand, and the physical activities of arrangement and rearrangement of complexities on the other.

By attributing a positive quality to potential energy, by identifying it with psychic energy which produces activities analogous to the psychic activities found in the higher animals and man, Teilhard is able to present a coherent explanation of development at every level based on scientific foundations, and at the same time avoid a mechanistic approach which would be based on complexity itself. In referring to the fundamental energy as psychic energy, Teilhard is not merely replacing old ideas with new names. As already noted, the physicist's concept of potential energy is derived entirely from the consequences of potential energy and is not concerned with the source or nature of this energy. A body is said to have potential energy because of what it is able to do. The actual nature of this potential energy in the body is left as an unknown factor. By calling the fundamental energy psychic energy, Teilhard actually gives a value to this unknown factor; that is, he states that the fundamental energy is actually consciousness and affinity. Since, however, the within of things, which is this consciousness and affinity, is not a separate entity but an aspect of all material bodies, Teilhard avoids dualism and any extreme forms of vitalism.

CHAPTER THREE

# The Hyperphysical Theory of Evolution

In Chapter One we said that hyperphysics is based on natural science and is an extension of natural science. In Chapter Two we have presented an interpretation of Teilhard's theory of energy—an interpretation which is in the spirit of hyperphysics for the following reasons: It shows Teilhard's concept of energy to be based on the physicist's concept of energy. It shows that his concept of energy is an extension of the physicist's. It should be noted that no vital principles or mysterious entities are added to reality; material bodies (including man) are complexities with energy. The hyperphysical extension gives a new interpretation of energy inasmuch as it explains energy in terms of consciousness and affinities ('love'), but the psychic energy whose nature Teilhard discusses is the same energy that the physicist measures.

In this theory of energy we have the basis of the Teilhardian explanation of the mechanism of the evolutionary process. This explanation is based on the scientific theory of evolution; however, because of the emphasis on psychic energy, Teilhard analyses evolution, not in terms of complexity alone, but in terms of complexity and consciousness.

In this extension of the theory of evolution, evolutionary development is a gradual and homogeneous process in which, as explained above, psychic activity brings about the formation of new arrangements. These new arrangements have new psychic activities which, in turn, lead to still further and more complex arrangements, and so on. From the level of the electron and proton to the level of the primate, there is a gradual development of complexity and an inter-related development of consciousness, and the mechanism of this process is the same throughout.

In spite of this homogeneity and continuity, nevertheless, there are certain points in the process, which Teilhard calls thresholds, at which small increases in complexity result in the development of radically new types of psychic activity. The increase in complexity brought about by the synthesis of nucleic acid and protein, for example, is, in itself, no more significant than any other increase in complexity. And yet, it leads to the development of very different activities—the activities of living organisms. (Activities so different, in fact, that until recently the possibility of life evolving from non-life was considered unthinkable.)

Although the development of complexity and the develop-ment of consciousness are really just two aspects of the one evolutionary process, nevertheless a small increase in complexity (and hence a small amount of tangential energy of arrangement) can be associated with a large increase in consciousness, or radial energy. The most obvious and important thresholds, at which such changes in radial energy have been initiated, are the threshold of life, and the threshold of thought (that is, the origin of man).


LIFE

The significance of the origin and development of life is discussed at length by Teilhard,[1] and so we do not intend to go into the question in detail here. We will, however, summarize some of Teilhard's more important conclusions.

Unlike non-living things, living organisms "leave a way continually open for a further increase of complexity and unified heterogeneity."[2] The organism's complexity is not arrested at its own level, but rather it can modify its own complexity without "unravel-ling". The unit remains closed in on itself, but the enclosure is mobile. The non-living water molecule, for example, retains the same basic arrangement as long as it is a water molecule. The living organism,

[1] See especially: THE PHENOMENON OF MAN, Book Two; and MAN'S PLACE IN NATURE, chapters 1 and 2.
[2] MAN'S PLACE IN NATURE, p. 31.

on the other hand, varies its arrangement from within while at the same time retaining its fundamental unity; it has, according to Teilhard, a "centricity" of action which distinguishes it from non-life.

This development of a new kind of "centricity"—a new and greater concentration of radial energy, is on the main axis of the evolutionary process. Life is not an epiphenomenon.

"Without any doubt, one portion of the cosmic stuff not only does not disintegrate but even begins—by producing a sort of bloom upon itself—to vitalise. So true is this, that besides entropy (by which energy is dissipated), besides expansion (by which the layers of the universe unfold and granulate), besides electrical and gravitational forces of attraction (by which sidereal dust conglomerates), we are now forced (if we really wish to cover the whole of experience and include the whole phenomenon) to envisage and admit a constant perennial current of 'interiorising complexification' that animates the whole mass of things."[1]

Evolution is, then, not merely the process of expansion and dissipation seen at the level of physical development. It is, in its living phase, a process of infolding—of concentration of energy—of convergence. This is seen more clearly in the development that follows the next major threshold: the threshold of reflection.

DEVELOPMENT OF THE NOOSPHERE

From the level of the electron and proton up to the level of the primate, there is a gradual development of complexity and an interrelated development of consciousness, the more complex beings having a more extensive awareness of their environment, and a subsequent increase in affinities for objects in their environment. It may be noted, however, that the objects of this increased awareness in the organisms below man are outside the consciousness itself; in other words, consciousness is not itself an object of consciousness. At some point in the evolutionary process, however, and probably due to a very small change in complexity, consciousness turned back upon itself and became its own object. Thus at the threshold of self-consciousness, or reflection, we find the origin of man, the rational animal. The non-self-conscious, or non-reflecting animal has little individuality. Its whole self is sub-

[1] *Ibid.*, p. 33.

merged in the group, able only to look outward. Consequently, un-aware of its own energies, affinities and aims, it develops blindly for the good of the species, the phylum, the whole evolutionary process. Man, through reflection, looks inward at his own powers, inclinations and goals, and in doing so, he takes on a new identity. The evolutionary process is no longer blind, nor is it simply a development of the masses. There is, within the species man, an increased emphasis on self resulting from self-consciousness, a kind of internal granulation as Teilhard puts it. This granulation does not, however, lead to a divergence of isolated individuals which would bring evolution to a halt. The self-conscious individual not only knows, but also knows that he knows. He can, consequently, know himself as self, thus increasing his own identity, and also can know another as other, bringing about a new intentional union. Furthermore, through this truly human knowledge, truly human love becomes a reality, and with it the highest degree of affinity in the evolutionary process.

Man, because of his ability to reflect, is the most centred being on earth. Self-consciousness enables him not only to centre himself upon himself, but also to centre all others upon himself. That is to say, man not only is able to reflect upon himself, but can also reflect upon his knowledge of others around him, thereby attaining a deeper comprehension than would be otherwise possible, and also a greater contact with his world. He becomes, therefore, a centre of centres.[1] Rather than leading to a divergence of isolated individuals, this leads to the second major stage in the process of development of self-consciousness. Following the threshold of the individual through the advent of reflection, there is a step which Teilhard refers to as the threshold of the phylum, the hominization of the species, or the convergence of the self-conscious granules.[2]

Teilhard indicates a number of causes of this unification or convergence. The increase in population on our planet will necessarily cause convergence; Teilhard calls this "geological curvature". Further unification will necessarily come about because of the universality of ideas, referred to as "mental curvature". Teilhard insists, however, that neither the physical proximity imposed by increased population in a limited space, nor the unity of ideas imposed by a community of scientists and advanced communications, is sufficient to produce

[1] Cf. THE PHENOMENON OF MAN, p. 258ff.
[2] Cf. THE PHENOMENON OF MAN, p. 174ff.

complete convergence. True unity will come about freely, through love; through an attraction to a common destiny freely accepted by all.[1]

According to Teilhard, the second stage in the development of the self-conscious layer, or "noosphere", has already begun. There is definite evidence of convergence because of geological curvature and mental curvature, and what is more important, in spite of the obvious divergences that exist on our planet, there is evidence of a developing human love of global proportions.

Convergence has begun, but it may take millions of years to complete. The ultimate result will be a perfect and permanent union among the individual human elements. This requires an irreversible evolution, and further analysis of the process gives evidence that such is the case. The argument for irreversibility may be summarized as follows:

Coherence, as we have seen, is Teilhard's criterion for truth. Accordingly, the most coherent view of the universe is the most true. The view of a continuous development of complexity-consciousness is the most coherent view, and therefore most closely approximates the truth. From this it follows that the production of life, or self-conscious man, and of socialization and the development of the thinking layer or the noosphere, are all essential and integral parts of the one whole continuous process of evolution. Rational and social development is not an epiphenomenon, but is as much a part of the process as is physical and chemical development. A fundamental unity of mechanism and structure exists throughout this process from bottom to top.

The development of the thinking layer or noosphere, from this point of view, is as much a biological development as is the development of the lower forms of life. (Teilhard even refers to the Incarnation as "a prodigious biological operation".) The development of the noosphere must, therefore, follow the same laws of development as do the lower levels of evolution if the whole process is to retain its coherence.

Reflecting on the lower levels of development we see that, as a general rule, the conditions for the fulfilment of a particular nature have existed and do exist. An appetite or tendency develops only in association with the object of that appetite or tendency. Electrons have protons to attract and be attracted to. Herbivores develop because

[1] Cf. THE FUTURE OF MAN, Ch. 20.

grass exists, and birds because there is an atmosphere in which to fly. An appetite without its corresponding object would be incoherent in nature. Inasmuch as the object cannot satisfy the appetite, development is retarded.

Teilhard applies this general rule of physical and biological development to the level of human development. Man knows the future and desires a future. He is a creative creature who wants not only well being, that is, that which will maintain him in his present state, but also desires to transcend his present state of being; he desires, in other words, more-being. As consciousness develops this will be increasingly the case. Man, therefore, with no future, with no prospect of more-being, would be as incoherent as the herbivore without grass, or the bird without air.

Within the context of Teilhard's principle of the unity of mechanism and structure this same argument may be restated in terms of radial or love-energy. As just stated, the actual existence of an attractive being is necessary before an attraction can take place. The electron is attracted to the proton because of the psychic energy of the electron and the existence of the proton. The rabbit is attracted to the carrot because of the psychic energy of the rabbit and the existence of the carrot. If there is an attraction there must not only exist the being attracted with its psychic energy, but also the being to which it is attracted with its capacity for fulfilment as a term of the attraction. Love, the manifestation of radial energy, is the affinity of being for being.

If then, the mechanism of evolution on the human level, or the level of the noosphere, is basically the same as at all other levels, the existence of a love for a future of more-being is an indication that this future of more-being will exist. Without its existence, human evolution would come to a halt, since its mechanism would lack an essential element.

It is, consequently, from an analysis of evolution as a development of complexity-consciousness that Teilhard concludes to its continued development to a terminal point, which he calls Omega. The following passage presents this important part of hyperphysics in Teilhard's own words: "By the nature of the work, and correlatively by the requirement [exigence] of the worker an unscalable wall, on which consciousness would crash and then for ever disappear, are thus "incompossible" with the mechanism of the activity of reflection (which would immediately break its mainspring). The more man becomes man, the less will he be prepared to move except towards that which is interminably and indestructibly new. Some "absolute" is implied in the play of his operative activity. If progress is a myth, that is to say, if faced by the work involved we can say: 'What's the good of it all?' our efforts will flag. With that the whole of evolution will come to a halt—because we are evolution."[1]

Teilhard adds in a footnote to the above that "all conscious energy is, like love (and because it is love), founded on hope".[2]

The concept of an "absolute", and the possibility of evolution tending towards the absolute, discovered by an analysis of the mechanism of human evolution, is further developed by Teilhard through his theory of a converging noosphere. Through reflection and love the self-conscious elements are converging upon themselves. This infolding of mankind upon itself is, for Teilhard, a fact beyond dispute. If, however, the elements of the noosphere are converging upon themselves, they are possibly also converging upon a common centre, a centre of centres, or a focal point.[3]

In the eyes of Teilhard, therefore, the evolutionary process will continue with man as its spearhead. The existence of self-consciousness will lead to an accelerated development of psychic energy, and also, in association with truly human love, will lead to an ultimate convergence of the human species. This development of consciousness at the human level is still associated with development of complexity and with new arrangements; however, as seen above, a high degree of psychic activity may be associated with a very small amount of physical energy. As development continues therefore, psychic energy becomes more and more prominent and physical energy becomes almost negligible. The whole evolutionary process then, is seen to be more a development of consciousness than a development of complexity. In other words, although all development involves the interaction of the two aspects of energy, radial and tangential, the radial aspect develops at a greater rate than the tangential aspect, and this is particularly evident at the level of man, where the development of radial energy is rapidly accelerated.

Two conclusions may be immediately drawn from this

---

[1] THE PHENOMENON OF MAN, pp. 230-1.
[2] *Ibid.*
[3] Cf. 'La Réflexion de l'Energie', in L'ACTIVATION DE L'ENERGIE, p. 351.

interpretation of the evolutionary process and both of these conclusions lead to serious problems in the Teilhardian synthesis. First,
evolution is viewed as a directed process—directed not only towards
the development of greater complexity but, more essentially, directed
towards the development of greater consciousness. The process is,
therefore, orthogenetic, and Teilhard admits this. This is a problem
in Teilhard's synthesis inasmuch as many biologists and evolutionists
today reject the concept of orthogenesis as applied to evolution.
Secondly, since, Teilhard sees an ultimate development for evolution
through the final convergence of the human species, the process is,
for him, an irreversible one. This is a problem since, according to the
prediction based on the law of increasing entropy, the evolutionary
process is reversible. These problems are especially critical since they
involve a discrepancy, and a seeming incompatability, between
Teilhard's hyperphysics and modern scientific theory; and if hyperphysics is to be an extension of science, and based upon good scientific
theory, such incompatabilities and discrepancies must be resolved.
These problems will now be discussed, beginning with the more
general problem of orthogenesis.

THE PROBLEM OF ORTHOGENESIS

The word orthogenesis is derived from the Greek orthos meaning
straight, and genesis meaning origin or birth, from gignesti—to become
or to be born. Etymologically, orthogenesis is therefore a becoming or
development in a straight line. The word, however, has taken on a
number of different connotations which, although related to the root
definition, may signify widely divergent views of evolution.

First, orthogenesis may mean simply that evolution has some
direction, or follows some path more or less straight, more or less
limited; evolution is not completely random. Inasmuch as it leaves
room for some random motion and meandering, some accidents,
"dead ends", and even regressions, this definition should be acceptable
to most Darwinians.

The term orthogenesis may also refer to a determined evolution following a well defined line within rigid limits. This definition,
like the first, is descriptive, but leads directly to the teleological
concept of a set goal, and a tendency towards that goal. It is related,

therefore, to a third use of the term orthogenesis which connotes a kind of causality insofar as it refers to an inner urge, a mysterious vital force, or a non-physical directing factor, which causes evolution to follow a straight-line path.

The second meaning of orthogenesis may have suited an earlier, simplified picture of evolutionary development, but cannot be applied today. Evolution is no longer pictured as a tree with a main trunk and a few well defined branches steadily growing upward, but rather as a tangled bush, which although in general growing up, has shoots sprouting in all directions, as well as dead ends.

The third definition, that is, the one which includes the concepts of a definite goal and of a vital principle leading towards that goal, would be rejected for the same reason as the second, and also because of the inclusion of the vital principle. The Darwinian explanation of evolution relies heavily on chance and on the influence of factors which are outside of the developing being—in other words, on ectogenesis, and hence it would conflict with any concept of a determined and autogenetic evolution as is found in this last definition. This definition is the most common connotation of the word.[1] Dobzhansky, for example, uses the term to refer to theories in which purposefulness is a property of life itself, a kind of autogenesis in which the potentiality existing in things is gradually unfolded in a manner which suits the existing environment. He says further that it is unfortunate that Teilhard speaks of evolutionary development as orthogenesis, and that this indicates a lack of knowledge of biology on Teilhard's part.[2] Dobzhansky, apparently, feels that Teilhard uses the term in the third sense as defined above. The following discussion of the meaning of orthogenesis in Teilhard will show that this is not entirely true.

Teilhard was well aware of the problems involved in the use of the term orthogenesis. He states that "on the pretext of its being used in various questionable or restricted senses, or of its having a metaphysical flavour, some biologists would like to suppress the word 'orthogenesis'. But my considered opinion is that the word is essential and indispensable for singling out and affirming the manifest property of living matter to form a system in which 'terms succeed each other experimentally, following the constantly increasing values of centro-

---

[1] See, for example, Huxley, EVOLUTION IN ACTION, p. 35; Blum, TIME'S ARROW AND EVOLUTION, p. 180; and Simpson, THE MEANING OF EVOLUTION, p. 30ff.
[2] Dobzhansky, MANKIND EVOLVING, pp. 347 and 348.

E

complexity'."[1] He states elsewhere that because of certain unaccept-
able meanings of the term orthogenesis, such as "a quasi mystical
linearity of phyla" implying certain vitalistic or finalistic conceptions,
a respectable paleontologist cannot use the word without embarrass-
ment. It must not be rejected he says, but corrected and reintroduced
in a manner which will convey the important ingredient of a general
direction in evolution. Teilhard says that he himself uses this word in
its etymological sense, in the most general sense of a transformation
which is directed to some degree, and under some influence, whatever
it is. The notion of vectors must be applied to evolution in some way or
other.[2]

On the one hand, Teilhard recognizes the problems involved
in using the term orthogenesis, and distinguishes between unaccept-
able and acceptable meanings. On the other hand, however, because
of the importance he attaches to the direction of evolution, he refuses
to reject the term, and defines it in a very general and cautious way,
which would seem to be acceptable among Darwinians. The definition
that he uses is similar to the first definition above, that is, orthogenesis
means that evolution has some direction. He insists, further, that
orthogenesis is a general characteristic, a large scale effect of evolution,
and in no way implies absolute determinism at any level of
development.[3]

In spite of what Teilhard says about his use of the term
orthogenesis, it would seem that this theory of a directed development
of complexity-consciousness, involving psychic energy, or the within of
things, would indeed indicate that he uses the term orthogenesis in the
third sense stated above, that is, the sense that includes the concept of a
vital principle, and which is generally rejected. We have already discussed Teilhard's criteria for direction: the development of the nervous
system, and the corresponding development of consciousness. We must
now look more closely at his explanation of the mechanism of this
development in terms of the within of things, with an eye to discovering whether or not it is compatible with the generally accepted
Darwinian theory.

We stated above that the concept of orthogenesis is usually
related to the concepts of vitalism and autogenesis. It is also related to

---

[1] THE PHENOMENON OF MAN, p. 108.
[2] THE VISION OF THE PAST, p. 268ff; and THE APPEARANCE OF MAN, p. 140ff.
[3] Cf. THE VISION OF THE PAST, p. 49ff., and p. 249ff.

the now rejected theory of evolution proposed by Lamarck. We must, therefore, pay particular attention to Teilhard's use of orthogenesis, vitalism and Lamarckism. Before proceeding to this, however, some discussion of Lamarck, Darwin, and chance will follow by way of introduction.

The principles of Lamarck's explanation of evolution may be presented as follows:

1. Living organisms and their component parts tend continually to increase in size.

2. Production of a new organ results from a new need, and from a new movement which this need starts and maintains.

3. If an organ is used constantly it will tend to become highly developed, whereas disuse tends to degeneration.

4. Modification produced by the above principles during the lifetime of an individual will be inherited by its off-spring with the result that changes are cumulative over a period of time.

The concept that development results from an inner need may lead to the postulation of a vital principle as the source of this need, and hence, to some form of vitalism. It also implies that the change is brought about for the purpose of satisfying the need, and therefore is in a sense teleological. Furthermore, the concept of a development brought about by a purposive vital principle leads to the conclusion of a directed evolution, or orthogenesis. Thus, Lamarckian autogenesis is identified with the vitalism, teleology, and orthogenesis which are rejected by many evolutionists today. Apart from this, experimental evidence shows that acquired characteristics are not inherited, and consequently, the fourth Lamarckian principle would also be rejected.

The modern Darwinian theory is a more mechanistic explanation. Evolution is not brought about by the purposive activity of a vital principle, but by the accidental coming together of elements. A mutation may be produced by a chance absorption of energy, which brings about a chromosomal transformation. The change affected will be rejected or maintained through a process of natural selection which involves actions and reactions between the living thing and its environment, which also appears to be to some extent accidental. The emphasis in this theory is, therefore, on ectogenesis and chance, rather than on autogenesis and purpose.

After reading THE ORIGIN OF SPECIES, Karl Marx enthusiastic-
ally wrote that Darwin had destroyed teleology, and indeed there are
a great many philosophers and scientists today who think that a
teleological explanation is incompatible with modern Darwinian
theory. A finalistic theory, such as that of Hegel, which puts the
burden of explanation on the final cause, and leaves no room for
chance, would certainly be difficult to reconcile with the modern
theory of evolution. It seems moreover, that when many modern
thinkers refer to teleology they have this extreme rationalistic type in
mind. Causality itself has been identified with determinism probably
because of the development of mechanistic physics and philosophy,
which likewise left little or no room for chance occurrences. The determinism found in classical mechanics is not teleological, but rather a
stronger form of mechanical causation than may be found in quantum
mechanics. The tendency in science has been away from these deterministic, or rigidly mechanistic explanations and towards explanations
involving chance and probabilities. Throughout the scientific world,
however, the emphasis has been on mechanistic or efficient causality,
while teleology, in any sense of the term, appears to have no place.

Chance, used in its most radical sense, refers to that which
happens totally without cause, that is, to the absolutely spontaneous or
fortuitous. Another view of chance sees the chance event as causally
identical to the non-chance or determined event, the difference being
not in the causes themselves, but in our knowledge of them. In a third
meaning, chance presupposes the mutual interference of independent
lines of causation. This latter definition, which has been traditionally
accepted as the most realistic, is the most useful one for understanding
Darwinian chance. Let us consider, for example, the concept of chance
mutation in the light of this definition.

One series of events may bring about the existence of a
certain amount of radiation at a particular place, and at a particular
time. Another series of events may place a particular animal at that
same place at the same time. The coming together of these two series
of events may produce a chromosomal transformation in the animal
which in turn will bring about a change in its offspring. This is a
chance event, or accident, in the sense that the cause of the radiation
was not determined to bring about this mutation, nor were the causes
of the movement of the animal determined to bring it about. The
mutation was not, nevertheless, absolutely fortuitous or without cause.

The success of Darwin's theory, with its emphasis on chance, has no doubt been influential in bringing about the use of probability theory in many branches of science. In some cases, the swing of the pendulum has been complete: from the strict mechanistic determinism of classical physics, and the teleological determinism of rationalist philosophy, to the acceptance of chance as the complete and ultimate explanation. This is exemplified in Lord Russell's suggestion that man is nothing but an accidental collocation of atoms.

On the other hand, there has been a call for a more balanced view which would avoid the extremes of determinism, but which would accept the idea of organization or design. The biologist is not so sure that a complete explanation by analysis and reduction is possible, or that the activities of the living world can be explained entirely in terms of accidental collocations of elements. Teilhard attempted to present a scientific account of the mechanism of evolution which would avoid the extremes of mechanism, blind chance, and ectogenesis on one hand, and of vitalism, determinism, and autogenesis on the other.

Teilhard's explanation revolves around his concept of directed chance.[1] His use of the concept of chance arises from his acceptance of the Darwinian theory as the explanation of the mechanics of evolution. Changes come about not primarily because of a conscious or unconscious desire within the being, but because of outside effects, which well may be considered accidental, such as the action of radiation on the chromosomes. A chance event of this kind may be the cause of a change in the progeny of the being which has suffered the chromosomal alteration. According to the Darwinians themselves, however, the change will be maintained or rejected within the species, depending on the interaction of the progeny and its environment. For example, a chance chromosomal change in a tiger may produce elongated fangs in its offspring. Given a tiger's environment, the elongated fangs will be beneficial, enabling the tiger to survive longer and produce more progeny. Here the emphasis is on ectogenesis, on external influences which are accidental and are beyond the control of the tiger itself. A further question may be asked, however, which leads to the notion of directed chance, and to Teilhard's Lamarckism: Why is it better for a tiger to have elongated fangs? or: Why is this change maintained within the species whereas

[1] For an introduction to this concept of directed chance cf. THE PHENOMENON OF MAN, p. 74 and p. 108ff; THE FUTURE OF MAN, p. 98ff and p. 217; THE APPEARANCE OF MAN, p. 139.

others are rejected?

In answer to this question, one might say that it is better for a tiger to have elongated fangs because a tiger "wants" to eat meat, or needs to eat meat to survive. This inner desire or urge is necessary. If a tiger were indifferent towards meat, or preferred a vegetable diet, or had no appetite for food at all, longer fangs would be superfluous, and their development within the species would not come about. Looking at the individual tiger, one may correctly say that he eats meat because he has fangs, and has fangs because of an accidental mutation. Looking at the species, however, one may say that tigers have fangs because they eat meat. The novelty produced by the chance mutation is, according to Teilhard, psychically selected by an inner urge, which finds its source in the within; in other words, the tiger's awareness of meat, and its affinity for meat are necessary elements in the process of evolution of the tiger. No reference is made to any mysterious entity in the being, apart from its body, but rather to the psychic energy which is a necessary aspect of all material bodies.

The long term development then, is not just an effect of external forces, but also of the psychic activity of the developing being. Teilhard himself regards this aspect of his doctrine as Lamarckian.

The Lamarckian principle accepted by Teilhard is obviously not the principle of inheritance of acquired characteristics. The principle used is that the production of a new organ results from a new need, and from the new movement which this need initiates and maintains. But while Lamarck applied the principle to ontogenesis, that is, to the development of each individual being, Teilhard applies it to phylogenesis, that is, to the development of a large group of beings, over a long period of time. In an individual being, a new characteristic is explained by the Darwinian theory of chance and external forces, rather than by a new need in the individual. In the species, however, the selecting and the maintaining of a new characteristic is explained by the needs of the species which are fulfilled by the psychic activity of each member.

The meaning of the word 'need' is very important in this context. The word 'need' may refer to a lack of something which is useful or necessary; or to the thing itself which is necessary; or to the demand or desire for the thing which is necessary. There has been a tendency to interpret 'need' in Lamarck's theory of evolution as a demand or desire. This interpretation emphasizes the role of the living organism as the active agent in the production of a new organ, and overlooks the function of external conditions; it leads to the autogenetic explanation. If, on the other hand, need is taken to refer to the lack of something useful, the organism is seen to be a more passive element in the production of new organs, and the emphasis may be shifted to external agents, and therefore to an ectogenetic explanation. In the Teilhardian context the use of 'need' would seem to include both of these meanings. (The same may be true of Lamarck's intended use of need.) New organs result from mutations produced by the action of external agents upon the organism. The need does not produce the new organ. If the new organ is not useful, or in other words, if there is no need for this organ, and no "demand" for it, the organ will not be selected and will not develop within the species. If, however, the new organ is needed it may be selected and may develop within the species. According to Teilhard the organism "recognizes" and "selects" that which is useful. The autogenetic element in the process is this psychic selection.

The terms "recognition" and "selection" do not, of course, refer to a conscious recognition of the new organ as such, nor the conscious selection of a new organ because it is recognized to be useful. Selection here is Darwinian selection with added emphasis on the psychic nature of the organism. For example, rabbits have developed powerful hind legs because rabbits need them for running, and must run to survive. The strong legs were actually produced by a series of mutations, but were selected because they were useful, and were useful because the rabbit has a natural tendency to survive and to do those things, such as run, which will enable it to survive. If the rabbit had no inner urge to survive, or run to survive, the strong legs would be of no use and would not be selected in the species. In this case, then, no conscious desire to have strong legs exists; the source of strong legs is found in a series of chance mutations, and an inner urge to act so as to survive. This latter factor is the psychic element in selection.

Teilhard refers to this psychic-selectivity as 'Lamarckian anti-chance'. This selectivity becomes more predominant at the higher levels of evolution where psychic activity is most developed; it cannot be seen directly at lower levels. He states, in fact, that the Darwinians probably are right in claiming that in the pre-human zones of life nothing but the play of chance selection is detected, but at the level of man the forces of internal arrangement are clearly seen in the process of evolution. For Teilhard, this amounts to saying that biological purposiveness is not everywhere apparent in the living world, but that it shows itself only above a certain level. And the truly purposive activity at the level of man, of course, would be due to the existence of self-consciousness. Even at the level of man, however, Lamarckian anti-chance or autogenesis still plays a relatively minor role as a mechanism of evolution when compared with Darwinian chance. Nevertheless, autogenesis is considered to be an essential ingredient of the whole evolutionary process, for although it is the reflective human zone which Teilhard regards as explicitly Lamarckian, this zone is the natural development of the pre-reflective layers of evolution. Accordingly, traces of Lamarckian anti-chance are found at lower levels; wherever beings have a within autogenesis is possible, and for Teilhard, the within is co-extensive with material complexity. All beings have a propensity to develop according to their own nature, and the source of this propensity is the psychic energy of the within.

These autogenetic tendencies themselves, however, are to a great extent at the mercy of the external world, and chance. No conscious effort on the part of the tiger can bring about the mutation which elongates its fangs, or the fangs of its offspring. This is produced by an occurrence over which it has no control, such as radiation or a biochemical reaction. Nor does it have much control over its surroundings—over, for example, the fact that it lives among animals upon which it can prey. All these factors come from outside the tiger, and make up the ectogenetic side of its development.

Nevertheless, the tiger's propensity for meat does come from within, and acting within the conditions laid down from outside, is an essential cause of development. The non-reflective being has, of course, no control over the appetite or affinity itself. The 'within of a carnivore' itself develops through an auto-ectogenetic process; it does not develop through a conscious desire on the part of a tiger to become a meat-eater. Man, a reflective being, is more or less aware of his affinities. He has, within certain limits, control over them and, accordingly, a greater control over his evolutionary development. The carnivore has no control over its appetite for meat, but man for any number of reasons may decide to become a vegetarian despite his desire for meat.

Although, according to Teilhard, Lamarckian anti-chance is not apparent at the lower ontogenetic levels of development, his statements that the earth was born by accident, that the planets were created by chance, and that God plays with chance, are founded on his belief in the existence of chance and design at every stage of evolution. Chance, for him, is a part of the general design of the evolutionary process in much the same way that chance is a part of the design of a card game, or game of dice. What is most evident at the atomic level is the accidental collocation. It is by chance, for example, that a particular electron unites with a particular proton to form a hydrogen atom. In other words, it would seem that particular protons are not determined to unite with particular electrons. Order is seen, in the fact that electrons unite with protons in a specific way. It could be said that this union depends upon the mutual awareness and affinities between electrons and protons; in other words, it depends upon their within.

The emphasis on chance in Teilhard's thought does not violate traditional principles of causality, nor does it eliminate the notion of necessity. In place of the absolute necessity of the determinist, Teilhard subscribes to the mathematico-physical concept of statistical necessity. He states, for example, that the improbable development of proteins leading to the origin of life was brought about by the play of large numbers.[1] The mathematical theories of statistics and probabilities have been closely associated with game theories, and an example from a game of chance, such as dice, may help to clarify the meaning of statistical necessity. If one dice is thrown it is said to be by chance that one particular number shows up. Knowing the design of the dice and the physical laws brought into play, one can calculate the chance as one in six. Similarly, the chances of different combinations of numbers, say "snake-eyes", may be calculated if a pair of dice is thrown. Since there is just one chance in thirty-six of getting snake-eyes in one toss of two dice, the appearance of this combination could not be considered to be a necessary event. If, however, one had a large number of dice, say 1,000, and furthermore, if they could be thrown a large number of times, then the chances of not getting this combination would be so small that one could say that its occurrence was inevitable or necessary. There would be, in fact, many of these combinations. This is not absolute mathematical necessity, but "practical necessity"; that is to say, it is so probable that it may be considered necessary "for all practical purposes".

The combinations required for the development of a protein molecule are infinitely more complex than the dice combinations in the

[1] THE FUTURE OF MAN, p. 290.

example. For this reason Teilhard refers to them as improbable in the mechanistic sense (and also from the point of view of the second law of thermodynamics). Given, however, the number of elements available for these combinations, the length of time available for them to take place, and the fact that the complex combinations are formed not in one step but in a series of less complex and therefore more probable steps, it is generally accepted that the occurrence of the combinations was statistically necessary. (This is a point that has been overlooked in arguments against the chance occurrence of complex organisms, such as used by William Paley, Lecomte de Nouy and Garrigou-Lagrange.[1])

Within the context of Teilhard's thought, the statement that God plays with chance may be interpreted as a rejection of a deterministic universe like that of Hegel or Laplace, or even the determinism that could develop from Lamarckism. It advances the belief in a world in which things with certain natures leading to certain activities act as secondary causes producing effects which are not absolutely necessary. God does not interfere in every particular bit of development, nor does each particular bit of development have a specific purpose in the mind of the Deity, as was taught by some of the teleologists. For example, we do not have eyes in order that we may see, but rather we see because we have eyes. Eyes were not created explicitly and immediately by a single creative act of God so that man could see. The existence of eyes is explained in terms of a long and complex process of events, none of which in itself was determined to produce the eye for the purpose of seeing. Nevertheless, for Teilhard, the process is intelligible only if its general purpose is recognized throughout, and at each and every step. In the light of Teilhard's thought this general purpose may be said to be the production of beings most suitable for their total environment, and this indeed is a very Darwinian concept. Darwin states that, "Owing to the struggle for life, any variation, however slight and from whatever cause proceeding, if it be in any degree profitable to an individual of any species, in its infinitely complex relations to other organic beings, and to external nature, will tend to the preservation of that individual and will generally be inherited by its offspring."[2] With reference to the above example, each step in the

---

[1] Cf. William Paley, NATURAL THEOLOGY, Indianapolis, Bobbs-Merrill, 1963, passim. Lecomte du Nouy, HUMAN DESTINY, N.Y., Longmans, Green, 1947, Ch. 3. R. Garrigou Lagrange, GOD: HIS EXISTENCE AND HIS NATURE, St. Louis (and London), Herder, 1955, Vol. 1, p. 351.

[2] Darwin, ORIGIN OF SPECIES, Ch. III (p. 53, Thinker's Library ed.)

development of light sensitive organs, from the most rudimentary to the most sophisticated eye, came about because it gave the organism in question a slight advantage whereby it became more suitable for living in, and coping with, its environment.

Given this general account of Teilhard's use of Lamarckism and his associated teleology we will now comment briefly on the value and acceptability of his theory. First, it may be noted that some of those who have criticized Teilhard for being too Lamarckian have assumed that he used Lamarck's principle of inheritance of acquired characteristics. For example, P. F. Forsthoefel, a Jesuit biologist, states this explicitly and goes on to say that Teilhard did not favour the modern genetical theory of evolution.[1] The Teilhardian text[2] that he uses to substantiate this position would appear, however, not to refer to Lamarck's principle of inheritance of acquired characteristics but rather to the psychic selection discussed above. In this text Teilhard states that the analysis of evolution in terms of chance, heredity and selection is not complete and suggests that a place should be left open for the effects of consciousness (that is, psychic selection) in the mechanism of evolution. Teilhard goes on to say that definitely there is a mechanistic aspect to the development of life; but he asks, is this development absolutely mechanistic?[3]

In the last paragraph of this same article, Teilhard suggests that the invention seen at the level of human development existed as a factor in the earlier stages of evolution. Out of context it may appear that in using the term invention Teilhard is accepting Lamarck's principle that a new need produces a new organ in the individual. Within the Teilhardian context however, the term invention would better be understood in its etymological meaning of discovery. In other words he is saying that man, and quite possibly lower forms of life, discover through consciousness the new perfections produced through mutations, and make use of them. This again is his principle of psychic selection.

We may compare this notion of invention and Teilhard's

---

[1] P. F. Forsthoefel, 'Beneath the Microscope', in, R. T. Francoeur (ed), THE WORLD OF TEILHARD, Baltimore, Helicon Press, 1961, p. 106.
[2] 'Evolution Zoologique et Invention', in LA VISION DU PASSÉ, p. 331 (THE VISION OF THE PAST, p. 234ff.)
[3] La Vie, incontestablement, monte des automatismes qu'il nous faut scientifiquement comprendre. Mais les montt-elle absolument automatiquement? Toute la question est là. *Ibid.*

insistence on the existence of psychic activity as a vital principle of natural selection, with the position of a noted biologist, Theodosius Dobzhansky: "The modern evolutionists believe that evolution is a creative response of the living matter to the challenges of the environment. The role of the environment is to provide opportunities for biological inventions. Evolution is due neither to chance, nor to design; it is due to a natural creative process."[1]

This is precisely Teilhard's view of the evolutionary process, and his theory of the psychic energy of the within is an attempt to explain this view. The within is the source of the creative response which brings about biological inventions; it is the active agent necessary in the process of natural selection.

Teilhard's concept of psychic selection is not an alternative to natural selection, nor does it contradict natural selection, but rather it is presented as a necessary ingredient of natural selection. Many members of the scientific community, however, think that the present theory of selection is a sufficient explanation of the evolutionary process, and would see this psychic element as superfluous. In this regard we may consider a statement by Sir Julian Huxley to the effect that the only effective agency of evolution is natural selection, and that all theories of orthogenesis, Lamarckism and mysterious vital forces are invalid.[2] As has already been admitted above, the modern theory of natural selection is incompatible with the principles of Lamarck, and with any extreme theory of orthogenesis, or vitalism. But, we have also said that Teilhard's use of Lamarckism and orthogenesis is compatible with natural selection. The question at hand is: does the acceptance of natural selection as the only effective agency of evolution rule out the possibility, or the necessity, of the addition of Teilhard's psychic selection; or is natural selection an effective agent because it includes a creative element such as found in Teilhard's theory?

The concept of natural selection, to have any real meaning, must refer to activities within the being itself, and mutual reactions between it and its environment. This is implicit in Darwin's own explanation of natural selection.[3] If a variation is useful or profitable for an individual member of a species in its complex relations with

[1] Dobzhansky, 'The Genetic Basis of Evolution' in SCIENTIFIC AMERICAN, January 1950.
[2] Julian Huxley, EVOLUTION IN ACTION, New York, Mentor, 1957, p. 35.
[3] Cf. Charles Darwin, THE ORIGIN OF SPECIES, Ch. III.

other organisms and its environment, then this variation will tend to preserve the individual and may be inherited by the offspring. The variation must be useful to the individual in its given condition to be selected; in other words it must satisfy a need.

Darwin's concept of natural selection has been developed to a great extent; nevertheless, the basic idea of natural selection remains the same and is considered to be the mechanism or agent which brings about evolutionary development. George Gaylord Simpson states that the orientation element of evolution is adaption, and the mechanism of adaption is natural selection. According to Huxley, mutation and recombination provide the raw materials for evolutionary change, and natural selection is the guiding or directive agency in that change. Sewall Wright thinks that no prominent geneticist now would question the essential validity of natural selection as the guiding principle of evolution.

But from the proposition that natural selection is the orienting element, guiding agency or guiding principle, does Huxley's statement that 'no conscious action is involved in natural selection' follow; or Simpson's that there can be no innate life tendency or progression toward a destined goal according to plan? Teilhard maintains that an innate life tendency is essential for the mechanism of natural selection as its orienting or guiding principle. If an awareness of the environment and an inner need did not exist, how could one explain the infinitely complex relations for the preservation of useful variations, of which Darwin speaks? Natural selection would not have developed a tiger's fangs unless, as Teilhard puts it, the tiger has 'the soul (or psychic energy, or within) of a carnivore.'

A criticism of Teilhard's Lamarckism presented by George Gaylord Simpson is also worth considering. In his review of THE PHENOMENON OF MAN, he says that Teilhard called the non-chance Lamarckian factors more important, even though he knew that most biologists consider these factors not only unimportant but non-existent. Simpson also states that the only objectively established anti-chance factor in evolution is natural selection, not Lamarckism.[1]

We have already maintained that Teilhard does not subscribe to all the Lamarckian factors but merely uses one of them in his own

[1] Cf. G. G. Simpson, in SCIENTIFIC AMERICAN, April 1960. This review was based on an early edition of the English translation in which the translation of 'psychique' was printed 'physical'. This distortion of Teilhard's thought apparently had some influence on Simpson's critique.

way. It is true that he refers to Lamarckian anti-chance, while Simpson points out that Darwinian selection is established as the anti-chance factor. Teilhard does not, however, see the Lamarckian element in opposition to the Darwinian element as Simpson suggests later when he says that Teilhard repeatedly contrasts selection with orthogenesis, treating them as opposites. What Teilhard does contrast is mutation as a chance event, and orthogenesis as design, and it is quite possible that Teilhard refers to the mutation factor in Darwinian theory when he speaks of Darwinian chance. Also, he could have in mind the chance aspects of natural selection, for example, the chance of being born in a particular place at a particular time, or the chance of meeting a particular mate or predator. His Lamarckian anti-chance is not, however, something apart from or opposed to natural selection, but along with the chance element it is a necessary part of it; it is the psychic element. If this point of view is correct it would be true to say that for Teilhard, the Lamarckian element is actually the anti-chance element of Darwinian natural selection.

The problem of teleological explanations is important enough to justify our dwelling on it a bit further. Possibly it is the abuse of teleology that has led to its being generally suspect today. We have already mentioned one such abuse: the argument that complex organisms cannot be produced by chance, based on the false assumption that these complex arrangements came about in one single step from their single components. Let us consider another common abuse.

It has been argued for example, that there is design and purposive activity because the following cannot be explained by chance: the earth is at the proper distance from the sun, has the proper rate of rotation, revolution and precession, and the proper atmospheric density to provide a climate suitable for human life. At first sight this type of argument is most convincing. And if more convincing is required, hundreds more such examples of purpose can be summoned. Further consideration shows, however, that the above example begs the question. It assumes that the earth was made for human life, and therefore assumes purposive activity. The fact is, probably, that it is because the earth has its particular climate etc. that human life exists. To say, 'the climate is proper for man' is not an accurate statement. Since man's evolution was partly determined, or conditioned by the climate, it would be more correct to say: 'man is one of the proper beings for this climate', rather than vice versa.

Teilhard did not abuse teleology; he sees that, in the theory of natural selection, consequences take over from purpose: 'we see because we have eyes', not 'we have eyes for the purpose of seeing'. To explain the consequences of natural selection, however, some overall purpose is necessary. This conclusion is not a result of the kind of basically semantic confusion as is found in the example above (or in Paley's use of the passive voice), but of an examination of the mechanism of natural selection in the context of Teilhard's theory of psychic energy.

In conclusion, to summarize we may say that Teilhard understands and accepts the basic principles and the explanation of the mechanism of evolution according to the Darwinian school. His theory of orthogenetic development with its Lamarckian principle does not contradict the Darwinian position; indeed, it is based on it. His inclusion of the within, and the inner need, has been seen to be the explanation of the creative aspect of natural selection, an aspect which has been recognized within the Darwinian school. Furthermore, his Lamarckism is no more than the inclusion of the within and its psychic selection as an integral part of the explanation of evolution. His concept of developing through directed chance, or statistical necessity, seems to be mathematically and scientifically acceptable. It presents a moderate view relative to the extremes of vitalism and teleology on the one hand, and mechanistic explanations through chance on the other. Teilhard would reject any theory of development based solely on purpose, and would also reject the concept that, in the light of modern biology, consequences have replaced purposes as an explanation. For him, purpose and consequence are inseparable elements of the complete explanation. On the level of ontogeny, we see because we have eyes. On the phylogenetic level, we have eyes in order to see. Individual variations arise from accidental mutations, but are retained in the species by being recognized as useful, and psychically selected, for the general purpose of producing organisms most suited to their environment. (By "recognized" here we do not refer to self-conscious recognition through which the object in question is actually known as good, or as useful, but simply the non-self-conscious awareness of, and the affinity for, those things which are good for the organism's proper development.) The result is an orthogenetic process, not in the sense that it is absolutely determined but rather in the sense that it is to some extent directed.

## THE PROBLEM OF ENTROPY

As we have already stated, Teilhard accepts the second law of thermodynamics as a valid physical law. Furthermore, since his hyperphysics is based upon physics, he also accepts it as a law which must
be reckoned with in his system. This immediately raises the problem of
the discrepancy between the physicist's forecast for the future of the
universe based on the second law, and Teilhard's forecast. We will now
discuss this problem, and Teilhard's proposed solution for it.

As we have seen above, the second law of thermodynamics
states that the total amount of energy available for new arrangements
in the universe is diminishing, and at some time in the future no more
available energy will exist. At such a time, therefore, the process of
evolution, which is a process of increasing complexity or arrangement,
will come to a halt, and reverse. The existing complexity will break
down, and there will be a regression towards complete disorder. View-
ing the universe as a whole, and in the light of the second law of
thermodynamics, the physicist sees this general tendency towards disorder as the main current of development. The evolutionary process
with its increase in complexity is seen as a smaller current, running
temporarily against the main current towards entropy. Evolution is
no more than a backwash or eddy in the irresistible tide towards
disorder.

Teilhard also recognizes these two currents, that is, the
current towards complete disorder, and the evolutionary current
towards greater complexity, and accepts that the latter runs counter
to the former. He sees evolution, however, not just as an increase in
complexity, but as a development of complexity-consciousness, and
furthermore, he sees the development of consciousness as the main
line of development. In other words, whereas on the one hand he
accepts the physicist's two currents, he rejects the physicist's evaluation
of their relative importance. Evolution as a development of consciousness and correspondingly greater complexity, is the main current; the
tendency towards greater entropy is secondary.

This shift in emphasis, however, does not in any way solve the
problem mentioned above; the fact still remains that increasing
consciousness requires increasing complexity, increasing complexity
requires energy, and according to the second law of thermodynamics,
the amount of available energy is decreasing. And so, Teilhard asks:

"Is it [radial energy] destined one day to start disintegrating so as to satisfy the principle of entropy, and fall back indefinitely into pre-living and still lower centres, by the exhaustion and gradual levelling-down of the free tangential energy contained in the successive envelopes of the universe from which it has emerged?"[1]

From the point of view of Teilhard's faith there is, of course, no problem. The Author of the law of entropy would not be subject to it, nor would that part of his creation for which he has willed ultimate perfection. Just as the death of the individual poses no threat to ever-lasting life, neither do the laws of thermodynamics. Teilhard, how-ever, wishes to arrive at the conclusion of an ultimate perfection of consciousness within a scientific context, that is, within his hyper-physics.

The only possible way to explain an irreversible process while accepting the second law of thermodynamics is to postulate a transformation in the future whereby the evolutionary process will escape from the law of increasing entropy. But this transformation must be explained within the scientific context; there is only one evolu-tion, insists Teilhard, and hence, any stage in the evolutionary process should be explainable in terms which are at least analogous to the terms used in the explanation of any other stage. Teilhard would not be satisfied with the idea of some special divine intervention as an ex-planation for the transformation which he predicts. If there is to be such a transformation it should be explainable in scientific terms.

For Teilhard, evolution is basically a continuous process of development of complexity-consciousness, with a fundamental unity of structure and mechanism throughout. But it is also a process which does produce qualitative novelty, that is, a process in which there are transformations giving rise to radically different beings, governed by new laws. The living is essentially different from the non-living, and consequently cannot be understood completely by the physicist through the laws of physics. The self-conscious is essentially different from the non-self-conscious, and as a result, man cannot be understood com-pletely by the biologist through the laws of biology. (It should be noted that the words 'radically different' and 'essentially different' are not used here in such a way as to imply that there is any discontinuity in the evolutionary process. We simply mean that at certain points in the one continuous process changes in structure occur which produce

[1] THE PHENOMENON OF MAN, p. 66.

F

relatively more radical changes in activity than at other points in the process.) In the light of a coherent picture of the whole evolutionary process it is possible, therefore, that in the future this process will cross a new threshold of being, beyond which some new laws will come into effect. Teilhard states that to the laws of conservation of energy, and degradation of energy (that is, increase of entropy), the law of reflexion of energy will be added.[1] The convergence, or reflexion,[2] of mankind upon itself will concentrate radial energy sufficiently for it to free itself from tangential energy.

This law of reflexion of energy, and the new being which gives rise to this law, will be a natural outcome of the whole process, and not something superadded. It will come about as naturally as did life and self-consciousness.

The development of this higher level of being in the future is consistent with Teilhard's position that radial energy, to which the law of increasing entropy does not directly apply, does exist at all levels of material being. Since the development of complexity-consciousness involves an increase or concentration of radial energy, a qualitative change can occur within the process. This transformation may be compared to others which appear to be analogous, and which can be explained by the physical scientist. For example, as the temperature of a liquid rises so does the kinetic energy of the molecules until, at a transformation point, that is, at the boiling point, the kinetic energy is sufficient to overcome the molecular forces which bound the substance together as a liquid. As another example: it has been theorized that at a certain stage in the early expansion of the universe gravitational forces took over from the forces of radiant energy, bringing about the formation of the galaxies.

These phenomena in which a transformation causes a change in the predominant law are commonplace in science. This might lead one to suspect that if development continues in the future as it has in the past, some transformations, unheard of today, may be expected, and associated with them, some new laws such as Teilhard's law of reflexion of energy.

Once again, the lack of development of Teilhard's concept of energy leaves his explanation of this transformation also somewhat

[1] L'ACTIVATION DE L'ENERGIE, p. 353.
[2] The word 'reflection' is used to refer to the power of consciousness to turn back upon itself. 'Reflexion' refers to the convergence or infolding of the noosphere. Cf. THE FUTURE OF MAN, "Translator's Note", p. 9.

vague. In the light of our interpretation of his concept of energy, however, we may look at the possibilities of a change in the second law of thermodynamics.

The physicist's forecast of a universe at maximum entropy, or complete disorder, is based on several assumptions, two of which we will mention here. It is assumed that the universe is an isolated system, that is, that there is no transfer of mass or energy into, or out of, the universe. (One statement of the second law of thermodynamics is the following: "The available energy of the isolated system decreases in all real processes.") This assumption has been questioned by some scientists who deny the validity of the second law; for example, the Reiser Vanderjagt model of the universe theorizes that around us, but not in our space-time matrix, is an ocean of electrical energy. There is a continuous transformation from this energy to matter, and back, though the process of transformation itself is a mystery. This process is regulated by a law which, it is suggested, could be identified with God. Such a model is of interest, since Teilhard himself sees God as the ultimate source of energy; however, Teilhard does not see God as a continuous producer of energy in the above sense, nor does he question the isolated universe assumption.

A second assumption, built into the physicist's forecast, is the assumption that the second law of thermodynamics will continue to apply indefinitely in the future. This is definitely the assumption that is questioned by Teilhard, and the consequences of this questioning must be considered. Without having recourse to miracles or some special divine interference, what would an escape from the second law of thermodynamics entail?

As we have seen, the fundamental reason for an increase in entropy in an isolated system is that heat energy cannot be completely reconverted into work. A total and continuous reconversion of heat energy to work would, therefore, abrogate the second law of thermodynamics. Such a change would be universal and fundamental and there is no evidence at present that such a change will take place. While it is true that some cosmological theories suggest a rebuilding of complexity, this rebuilding would take place after the dissipation and destruction of our present physical universe. In other words, the transformation would take place after the present forecast of the physicist had come true.

Another possibility, and one more in line with Teilhard's

statement that evolution will escape from entropy, is that at some time in the future evolution will be able to proceed without the intervention of an arrangement. With no further need of arrangement there would be no further need of energy of arrangement, and hence the process would escape from the second law. To analyse this idea, we will have to return to and further develop some of the concepts that have been presented above in our discussion of energy.

Although the parts of a complex being continue to function to some extent according to their own nature, or in other words appear to retain their own psychic energy, there is also, in the development of consciousness, a concentration of psychic energy. The activity of a complex being does not appear to be simply the sum of the activities of its parts, but rather there seems to be a unity of activity. The complex being acts as a unit, and this is what Teilhard refers to when he speaks of the concentration of psychic energy. Since psychic energy is not distributed and dissipated throughout the complex being, but is in some way centred, psychic energy becomes more concentrated as beings become more and more complex. This centring of psychic energy becomes more evident with the development of the brain, which is a centre of activity in living organisms, and becomes most evident in man where the individual human himself is aware of his identity and the unity of his operations.

In all development to date, complexity would appear to be a necessary, but not sufficient condition for the development and operation of psychic energy. As stated before, if complexity itself depends upon psychic energy it cannot be the fundamental cause of this energy, and hence is not a sufficient condition. We have also stated, however, that there is some experimental evidence to indicate that complexity is becoming less and less necessary as a condition for psychic activity. The higher psychic activities of man require less energy of arrangement than do some of the simpler activities. If it is correct to propose that there is an inverse ratio between the increasing concentration of psychic energy and the necessity of energy of arrangement, then an ultimate complete independence of psychic energy on energy of arrangement could be forecast. This forecast would certainly be in line with Teilhard's idea that evolution is primarily a development of consciousness, and secondarily a development of complexity.

Teilhard explains this development towards the independence of radial energy as follows: ". . . followed upward towards very large complexes, the same 'psychic' element from its first appearance in beings, manifests, in relation to its matrix of 'complexity', a growing tendency to mastery and autonomy. At the origins of life it would seem to have been the focus of arrangement (F1) which, in each individual element, engenders and controls its related focus of consciousness (F2). But, higher up, the equilibrium is reversed. Quite clearly, at any rate from the 'individual threshold of reflection'—if not before—it is F2 which begins to take charge (by 'invention') of the progress of F1. Then, higher still, that is to say at the approaches (conjectured) of collective reflection, we find F2 apparently breaking away from its temporo-spatial frame to join up with the supreme and universal focus Omega."[1]

At the lower levels of evolution, psychic energy has little control over development itself, and is to a great extent at the mercy of the forces of chance. At the higher levels, however, and particularly at the level of man, evolutionary development itself is to a large measure psychically controlled, and this for Teilhard is evidence of the autonomy of radial energy.

We spoke above of the law of reflexion of energy which would govern development in the future, just as the law of conservation of energy and the law of increasing entropy have governed development in the past. The law of reflexion of energy refers to Teilhard's idea that the development of consciousness will escape from the law of entropy by the effect of reflexion. Reflexion here does not refer to the self-consciousness of the individual human reflection, but rather to the convergence of the human species. The whole species is seen as a complex unit composed of individual humans as elements. As a complex unit, the species itself would develop a certain kind of radial energy. In other words, and as we have seen before, the individual energies of the members are not dissipated, but rather concentrated in the process of convergence.

It should be noted that energy itself, and hence radial energy, obeys the first law of thermodynamics, that is the law which states that energy can be neither created nor destroyed, but only converted from one form to another. Consequently, if the necessity of arrangement were eliminated, the continued existence of the fundamental energy would not be in jeopardy.

It must be made clear that the above discussion on the

[1] THE PHENOMENON OF MAN, p. 308.

possibility and nature of an escape from the law of increasing entropy is not to be confused with the forecast of this escape. The reasons for predicting the escape from entropy are, as we have seen, found in Teilhard's analysis of evolution of consciousness and especially of self-consciousness.

In conclusion, the following points should be noted: First the ultimate development and perfection of the universe, or at least of its human elements, was, of course, accepted by Teilhard as a part of his Christian faith. Believing as he did, however, in a fundamental coherence in the evolution of the universe, and rejecting a radical distinction between matter and spirit, Teilhard held that this ultimate development could be scientifically predicted, and scientifically explained. Neither the prediction nor the explanation are presented as absolutely certain. In some respects the arguments in favour of the prediction seem to be weaker and less scientific than the justification of the transformation which the prediction necessitates. It is not at all unreasonable to question the continued validity of the second law of thermodynamics, nor is it unreasonable, in the light of Teilhard's emphasis on the development of consciousness, to predict that psychic energy could eventually escape from the law of entropy. But, once again, to say that psychic energy could escape from the law of increasing entropy is not to say that it will escape.

# CHAPTER FOUR

# Is Hyperphysics Scientific?

Those who expect to find an answer to the above question in the pages that follow will be disappointed. We would not be so bold as to say that the preceding chapters have answered the question: "what is hyperphysics?" Nor are the philosophers of science bold enough to state that they have a clear and unanimous answer to the question: "what is the scientific method?" Because of the complexity of the problem even a tentative answer would require another volume; and so we must be satisfied here with a few comments which may help to clarify what has been said in the chapters above, may lead to further research into the question, and definitely will lead to more questions than answers.

Commentators on Teilhard have had difficulty in categorizing his work, and this might be expected for he looked upon science, as he looked upon reality, as a continuously developing homogeneous whole. He would, consequently, reject the classification of thought into air-tight compartments, and hyperphysics does not appear to belong to any one of the traditional categories of systematized knowledge (unless, possibly, we return to the concept of 'natural philosophy'). Teilhard admits that hyperphysics is not natural science as it is now understood. This does not, however, preclude the possibility that hyperphysics is scientific; but if we are to investigate this possibility we must be able to answer the question: what does 'hyperphysics is scientific' mean?

It would mean that hyperphysics uses the scientific method, or some acceptable extension or variation of the present scientific method; but since the nature and scope of the scientific method is itself the subject of much discussion today, and since Teilhard's method also needs further clarification, we could not possibly say the final word on this matter.

It would also have to mean that hyperphysics has scientific (or empirical) foundations. We have discussed the scientific basis of hyperphysics, and it is clear that it rests, for example, on the general theory of evolution. It is not as clear, however, that all of the principal elements of hyperphysics rest on empirical foundations. (Moreover, it is not perfectly clear what empirical foundations are.)

It would also have to mean (and this would be a minimum requirement or sine qua non condition), that the conclusions of hyperphysics are compatible with the accepted facts, laws and theories of modern science. This is the problem that we have considered to the greatest extent in this work, attempting to show compatibility between hyperphysics and the scientist's concept of energy, the second law of thermodynamics, and the modern Darwinian theory of evolution. To the extent that this attempt has been successful, we have at least started to answer the question: "Is hyperphysics scientific?" We will begin by briefly reflecting on what we have already said about the compatibility of hyperphysics with science.

First, the Teilhardian principle that all energy is psychic does not seem to contradict any established facts. The nature of the fundamental energies in the physical universe, that is, gravitational energy, electrostatic energy and nuclear energy is, as yet, unknown. But what is known is compatible with panpsychism. Regarding gravity for example, recent experiments at Princeton University lead to the conclusion that "gravitational effects—like electromagnetic ones—are due to the interaction of matter with one or more of three kinds of classical field", which possibly is "a single tensor field."[1] This field theory of gravity, and the field theories of electrostatic and nuclear forces, are compatible with Teilhard's concept of psychic energy. Insofar as a field is considered by the physicist to be an area of influence, or the space throughout which a force operates, field theories can be regarded as the quantitative descriptions of fundamental psychic activities.

Secondly, Teilhard does not contradict the generally accepted

R. H. Dicke, P. G. Roll and J. Weber; 'Gravity Experiments', in MODERN SCIENCE AND TECHNOLOGY, edited by Robert Colborn, Princeton, N.J., D. Van Nostrand Co. Ltd., 1965, pp. 3 and 4.

Darwinian-Mendelian theory of the mechanics of evolution. He recognizes chance mutations and natural selection as necessary elements in development. The Lamarckian principle which he uses is not the rejected principle of inheritance of acquired characteristics, but an amended concept of inner need, which is compatible with today's theory of evolutionary development.[1]

Thirdly, Teilhard does not contradict the generally accepted view that evolution follows a meandering complex of paths, resulting from the randomness of mutations and selection. Orthogenesis refers to a principal or privileged axis within the maze, which itself does not necessarily follow a straight and determined line.

Fourthly, Teilhard's theory of orthogenesis does not contradict the law of entropy, but, on the contrary, accepts it as a valid physical law which must be constantly kept in mind while looking into the future. Because of this he sees the necessity of a transformation in the future to free the radial from the tangential energy completely, and thus from the thermodynamic effects.

Fifthly, the concept of a within does not contradict any findings of modern science. A statement like Huxley's or Toulmin's that there is no scientific evidence for a within certainly does not rule out its existence. Teilhard recognizes that the within is not the object of present-day physical science, but this does not preclude the possibility, if not probability, of its being an object of physical science in the future. Accordingly, the concept of the within belongs to a hyperphysics.

Not only must a good theory be compatible with established facts and theories; it must also be without any internal contradictions. In keeping with this criterion the essential elements of Teilhard's hyperphysics show the self-consistency necessary for a good theory. He adheres to his principle of unity of mechanism and structure throughout, even to the point of presenting man's self-consciousness as a part of the continuous process of evolution, the development of society in terms of "divergence-convergence-emergence", and the Incarnation as a "prodigious biological operation". His consistency is evident, for example, when he admits the possibility of failure of the orthogenetic process leading to the destruction of the noosphere because of his acceptance of "Darwinian chance" as a mechanism of evolution at

[1] Cf. PROCEEDINGS OF THE TEILHARD CONFERENCE (1964), New York, Fordham University, p. 37.

every level from the atomic to the self-conscious.

Another very important consideration is the objective basis of the premises of a theory. It is not sufficient that a system be simply logically coherent. The systems of Descartes, Spinoza and Hegel are logically consistent, but inasmuch as they lack empirical foundations they are not considered to be satisfactory explanations of reality.

Scientific principles must have some objective foundation; they must, in other words, conform to reality. This is not to say, however, that the truth of the premises need be known. In fact, the premises of many acceptable theories in science are themselves of a highly theoretical nature, and therefore are not known to be true or false themselves. The premises of a good scientific theory must be compatible with established facts and must be supported either directly or indirectly by empirical evidence. Furthermore the evidence upon which they are based must be other than the evidence upon which the acceptance of the explicandum is based.

We have already discussed the first requirement, that is that the premises be compatible with established fact. Whether or not Teilhard's hyperphysics satisfies the second requirement is much more difficult to see. We will, nevertheless, consider this second require-ment, that is, that the premises be supported by empirical evidence other than that upon which the acceptance of the explicandum is based.

One of the major principles of hyperphysics is the principle of coherence, and definitely, any science must itself be a coherent system. No coherence, however, within a scientific system can be produced by logic alone and remain realistic. The coherence of the system must reflect an objective coherence discovered in reality; some unity and continuity must be found by the scientist in the diversity of the physical world sur-rounding him. To discover this unity and continuity in nature to permit the development of a coherent picture of the world is his principal task as a scientist. With regard to this point, Albert Einstein states: "Science is the attempt to make the chaotic diversity of our sense-experience correspond to a logically uniform system of thought. In this system single experiences must be correlated with the theoretic structure in such a way that the resulting co-ordination is unique and convincing.

The sense-experiences are the given subject-matter. But the theory that shall interpret them is man-made."[1]

[1] Albert Einstein, 'The Fundamentals of Theoretical Physics' (1940), in: OUT OF MY LATER YEARS, New York, Philosphical Library, 1950, p. 95.

Through the modern physical theory of evolution we have a picture of continuity on the level of complexity based on sense experience. Teilhard sees a more extensive coherence in which there is a continuity of complexity-consciousness. This continuity leads directly to the conclusion that there is a within and without at every level, and the activity of psychic energy throughout. A principle of continuity first formulated by Leibniz may be recalled in connection with this conclusion. This principle of continuity, "rests upon the impossibility of proper division of a uniform continuum. It is scientifically unsound to exclude, as Euclid does, the null angle and the straight angle from the notion of an angle."[1]

Similarly, if the universe is seen to be a continuum of comlexity-consciousness it would be scientifically unsound to divide the continuum so as to exclude psychic energy from some segment of it.

This conclusion is scientifically sound, however, only if the principle upon which it is based is scientifically sound. The scientific validity of Teilhard's principle of coherence must be considered. We may do this in the light of Newton's RULES OF REASONING IN PHILOSOPHY, He states the rules as follows: "Rule I: We are to admit no more causes of natural things than such as are both true and sufficient to explain their appearance."

This is based on the notion that Nature does nothing in vain, and accordingly, will not use more causes than are necessary. "Rule II: Therefore to the same natural effects we must, as far as possible, assign the same causes . . ." "Rule III: The qualities of bodies, which admit neither intensification nor remission of degrees, and which are found to belong to all bodies within the reach of our experiment, are to be esteemed the universal qualities of all bodies whatsoever."[2]

The continuity of the axis of complexity is, of course, based on the theory of evolution. The extension of the axis of consciousness from the uppermost levels of development to the lowest is not based directly upon empirical evidence, but it does follow Newton's rules. We know that certain activities of living beings, such as their awareness of their environment and their appetites, are psychic. We may, then, postulate psychic energy as the cause of similar activities whose causes

[1] Leibniz, quoted in: Hermann Weyl, PHILOSOPHY OF MATHEMATICS AND NATURAL SCIENCE, Princeton University Press, 1949, p. 160. Cf. also p. 155.
[2] Sir Isaac Newton, PHILOSOPHIAE NATURALIS PRINCIPIA MATHEMATICA, Motte translation (1729) revised by Cajori, Berkely, University of California Press, 1960, p. 398.

are at present beyond our grasp. In other words, a within exists at every level and evolution is a development of complexity-consciousness.

Consciousness is not evident at the lower levels of creation, and yet Teilhard insists that the physical scientist will eventually have to recognize it. The physical scientist, however, is at present concerned only with that which is empirically verifiable, or at least, empirically verifiable in principle. The general theory of evolution is not actually empirically verifiable, but since it deals with the development of complexity it is potentially verifiable by empirical means, or verifiable in principle. The proposition, "There is a continuous axis of complexity", is, therefore, scientific in the sense that it is empirically verifiable. On the other hand, consciousness cannot be empirically observed. Hence the proposition, "There is a continuous axis of consciousness coextensive with the complexity axis", is not empirically verifiable, even in principle. The proposition regarding consciousness is, consequently, not scientific in the same sense as is the proposition regarding complexity. Furthermore, if one limits science to strict empirical methods, then, according to such a definition Teilhard's parameter of consciousness is not orthodox science. Many scientists today, however, are in favour of a less rigid definition of the scientific method, or, in other words, of more "unorthodox" science.[1] Nagel, for instance, writes: ". . . the conclusions of science, unlike common-sense beliefs, are the products of scientific method. However, this brief formula should not be miscontrued. It must not be understood to assert, for example, that the practice of scientific method consists in following prescribed rules for making experimental discoveries or for finding satisfactory explanations for matters of established fact. There are no rules of discovery and invention in science, any more than there are such rules in the arts. Nor must the formula be construed as maintaining that the practice of scientific method consists in the use in all inquiries of some special set of techniques (such as the techniques of measurement employed in physical science), irrespective of the subject matter or the problem under investigation. Such an interpretation of the dictum is a caricature of its intent; and in any event the dictum on that interpretation is preposterous."[2]

This viewpoint would leave room within the field of science

---

[1] Cf. for example, R. G. Colodny (ed.), BEYOND THE EDGE OF CERTAINTY, Englewood Cliffs, N.J., Prentice-Hall, 1965, p. 4.
[2] Ernest Nagel, THE STRUCTURE OF SCIENCE, Harcourt, Brace & World, N.Y., 1961, p. 12.

for the inclusion of Teilhard's theories insofar as it permits deviation
from the strict empirical method. A more positive statement by Nagel
further justifies the inclusion of hyperphysical theory within the scientific spectrum; he defines scientific conceptions as: ". . . formulations
of pervasive structural properties, abstracted from familiar traits
manifested by limited classes of things usually only under highly
specialized conditions, related to matters open to direct observation
only by way of complex logical and experimental procedures, and
articulated with a view of developing systematic explanations for
extensive ranges of diverse phenomena."[1]

Teilhard's conception of consciousness as a property of all
material beings is abstracted from the familiar activities of a limited
class, namely man, and the higher animals. Its purpose is to develop a
systematic explanation for the most extensive range of diverse phenomena, and Teilhard's explanation is truly systematic. The relationship
between this concept and matters open to direct observation are by way
of logical rather than experimental procedures; for example, there
would appear to be no experimental evidence to show that psychic
energy causes a tree to send out tap roots, or a union of oxygen and
hydrogen. This in itself, however, should not bring about the exclusion
of Teilhard's theories from the world of science, unless it is held that
the empirical method must be used to obtain all scientific knowledge,
without exception.

The lack of experimental method in Teilhard's approach to
consciousness does not, in itself, result in a lack of certainty. We have
no experimental evidence of the consciousness of higher animals, and
yet we are certain of its existence. We observe that animals have
activities similar to our own, and since we know through reflection that
our consciousness and appetites are at the root of our activities, we
reason that animals have consciousness and appetites. According to
Teilhard, it is only our unfamiliarity with the activities of things
farther down the scale of evolution that makes us less certain of their
possession of psychic energy.

Since Teilhard's concept of consciousness is derived primarily
from man and then attributed to other things according to their degree
of development, this concept is analogical, the analogy being one of
proper proportion and the primary analogate being man. This is
entirely consistent with his principle of coherence through which he

[1] *Ibid.*, p. 11.

sees a uniformity, continuity and similarity throughout the material universe, but at the same time sees radical differences along the axis of development. With regard to the use of analogy in science we may quote further from Sir Isaac Newton: "We are certainly not to relinquish the evidence of experiments for the sake of dreams and vain fictions of our own devising; nor are we to recede from the analogy of Nature, which is wont to be simple, and always consonant to itself."[1]

This use of analogy in devising a theory is quite valuable in science, even when it is recognized that the theory may be modified by future experimental evidence. Weyl gives the following example: "We meet the principle of analogy in perhaps its most significant application in the establishment of the atomic theory. The mechanical laws, which had been derived from the behaviour of ordinary visible bodies and had been most precisely confirmed by the planets are carried over to atoms. One anticipates that the facts may later enforce corrections, but without this preliminary adoption of the mechanical laws no beginning of atomic research is thinkable."[2]

The scientist may also anticipate that the existence of the analogous perfection in the subject will eventually be proved, or disproved, experimentally. To one who insists that this be the case, once again Teilhard's theory falls outside the definition of science. If, however, diversity of method is permitted to bring about a systematic explanation with some degree of probability, then Teilhard's use of analogy may be scientifically acceptable.

From what has been presented above we can conclude that Teilhard's hyperphysics is not empirical science in the strict sense of word. That is, if empirical science is defined in such a way that only the experimental method may be used, and only concepts empirically verifiable may be considered, then his theory must be excluded inasmuch as it is based on principles that are not empirically verifiable and uses non-experimental methods. If, on the other hand, we accept the position that empirical sciences can, and possibly must at times deviate from a strict empirical approach if they are to develop, then we may classify Teilhard's theory as scientific. Energy is not in itself directly observable, but its existence is inferred by the physicist through the empirical observations of activities which it produces. We

---

[1] Newton, *op. cit.*, p. 398.
[2] Weyl, *op. cit.*, p. 161.

would not say however, that the concept of energy is not a scientific concept. It is, in fact one of the most fundamental of all scientific concepts. If, therefore, the relationship between energy on the one hand, and consciousness and love on the other is justified, these concepts should be considered just as scientific as the concept of energy.

It could be argued of course that the scientist recognizes the existence of something which he calls energy but makes no attempt as a scientist to explain its nature. He is satisfied simply with what it can do, how it operates, etc. To relate energy to consciousness and love would seem to be saying something about the nature of energy and statements about the nature or essence of things are not, according to many, scientific. This raises the whole problem of essentialism versus instrumentalism as opposed views of scientific theory. We might suggest that Teilhard's view of science would lie somewhere between essentialism and instrumentalism. He seems to believe that science can truly explain reality without assuming that this explanation involves going beyond the level of observation to some mysterious essential level. He would not accept, for example, the instrumentalist view of Berkeley who believed only in spiritual essences and therefore held that all explanation would involve God, and come from religion. Teilhard would agree that the ultimate explanation of reality is to be found in God and would also agree in a fundamental distinction between the creator and the created; however, he would not accept a similar distinction between a spiritual order and a material order within the created universe. The two aspects of material beings, that is, complexity and consciousness, are accessible to scientific investigation, and such investigation would lead to what one could reasonably call an explanation. (The connection between energy, and God or Christ in Teilhard's synthesis could form the ultimate explanation of reality, but this point would have to be studied further by competent theologians.)

We will conclude with a brief comment on the relationship between hyperphysics and philosophy, and theology. It has been suggested that hyperphysics is philosophical, and so, the following question immediately arises: In Teilhard's synthesis, does natural science "evolve" continuously into philosophy, forming a continuous spectrum of knowledge? In other words, does hyperphysics as an extension of science and a replacement for metaphysics form a new "natural philosophy"?

In answering this question we might take cognizance of what Maritain says about the difference between experimental science and philosophy. He maintains that a certain continuity or solidarity exists between the specifically rational part and the specifically experimental part of knowledge. Whereas the sciences at the lower end of the spectrum of knowledge, such as physics, still use an almost purely mathematical method, the sciences higher up the spectrum, such as biology, include a philosophical approach. Maritain states that, unlike physics, ". . . experimental biology and experimental psychology do not undertake to reconstruct a closed universe of mathematicized phenomena, and it is quite normal that the type of deductive explanation whose attraction they undergo should be of a philosophical type and not of a mathematical type."[1]

Teilhard would not deny that there are essentially different or radically different kinds of knowledge, any more than he would deny the existence of essentially different kinds of beings. For him, however, the existence of essentially different beings does not mean that evolution is discontinuous, nor that there is no unity of structure or mechanism, nor that there is a lack of coherence in the universe. This picture of the real world is reflected in his epistemology. Within hyperphysics both empirical methods and rational or philosophical methods are used, but it remains one continuous science, somewhat in the sense that Maritain speaks of continuity of science. The biologist, says Teilhard, has already recognized the existence of consciousness as a biologist, and to this extent, has already become a philosopher. Indeed, according to Maritain: ". . . it is only by using the equipment of the philosopher, by becoming philosophers themselves, that they (biologists and psychologists) will be able to give a proper and adequate solution to supraexperimental problems that their own experience compels them to envisage . . ."[2]

To state that Teilhard's thought evolves into the philosophical is not to say that it encompasses all philosophy. His philosophy does not comprise an explicit ontology nor an explicit epistemology and his theodicy is a natural or physical theology rather than a metaphysical theology. Although metaphysical principles are used, as they are in any science, there is no developed metaphysics. There are,

[1] Jacques Maritain, THE DEGREES OF KNOWLEDGE (translated by G. B. Phelan) London, Geoffrey Bles, 1959, pp. 64-65.
[2] *Ibid.*, p. 66.

however, philosophical starting points,[1] and philosophical methods such as deduction and analogy leading to some philosophical conclusions, the existence of Omega, for example.

Although we have not given a detailed analysis of Teilhard's concept of Omega, a note on the role of faith and theology in his synthesis may still be appropriate.

Separate from hyperphysics, the natural science, but converging with it, is Theology, the supernatural science. Faith and revelation do not, for Teilhard, form a part of hyperphysics, but constitute instead a separate knowledge which leads to the same conclusions as hyperphysics. From the convergence of the divergent knowledge through Faith and science emerges the total picture of reality.

The theory of convergence upon the Omega Point, discussed above, appears to be based on Teilhard's hyperphysical principles. Certain conclusions about the Final Cause, however are, for Teilhard, based on Faith. At the end of an analysis of socialization as an essential phenomenon of hominisation he states, for example: ". . . the human phenomenon, seen in its entirety, appears to flow towards a critical point of maturation, . . . corresponding to the concentration of collective Reflection at a single centre embracing all the individual units of reflection upon Earth.

Further than this we cannot see and our argument must cease—except . . . in the case of the Christian, who, drawing upon an added source of knowledge, may advance yet another step."[2]

The difficulty lies in attempting to define the line of demarcation between that part of Teilhard's theory which is based on phenomena and that part based on Faith. Within his total world vision, however, this should not be surprising. Just as one form of material being blends into the next within the continuous spectrum of the evolutionary process, so too one form of Teilhard's thought blends into another. The discussion of Omega may be considered to be on the borderline between phenomenology and Theology, just as the virus is on the borderline between non-life and life. He states, for

---

[1] Cf., for example, P. H. Van Laer, THE PHILOSOPHY OF SCIENCE (Part One), Pittsburgh, Duquesne University, 1956, p. 51. "The philosophical sciences have their starting point in an intellectual reflection on the general data of experience with respect to the being of man and things outside man". (See also this author's discussion of the starting points of other sciences, *ibid.*)

[2] THE FUTURE OF MAN, pp. 222-3.

instance: ". . . the Christian point of view [with regard to the unification of all men in God] . . . coincides with the biological viewpoint
logically carried to its extreme . . ."[1]

The above analogy between the Omega and the virus is
used merely to indicate the lack of defining limits within the Teilhardian synthesis. It does not imply that Teilhard's Faith or Theology
is a further development of his phenomenology. He arrives at the same
conclusion from two different directions. The study of the phenomena
leads Teilhard to probable conclusions which coincide with articles of
Faith about which he is certain. If, for example, the Pleroma does not
develop naturally through reflexion of the Noosphere, and this, according to Teilhard, is possible, Omega, or God, and the immortality of
man would still be facts for him. He accepts them as facts based on
Faith independently of his phenomenological synthesis. "If we would
form an idea of the active power of faith and of what it achieves we
must have struggled long and patiently: we must, in view of the
practical uncertainty of the morrow, have thrown ourselves, in a true
act of inward submission, upon Providence considered as being as
physically real as the objects of our disquietude; . . ."[2]

St. Thomas Aquinas, using the best philosophy available to
him and interpreting it for his own purposes, presented rational
demonstrations for the existence of the God whom he already knew
through his Faith. Teilhard, using the best in scientific theory available
to him, and interpreting it in his own way presents his theory of
orthogenesis which leads to the concept of Omega, which is the God
he knew from the beginning through Faith. There is a convergence of
Teilhard's theory of orthogenesis and Faith, but the two do not become
one until the concept of Omega-God is reached.

[1] *Ibid.*
[2] HYMN OF THE UNIVERSE, p. 131.

# Concluding Unscientific Postscript

In its review of the TEILHARD DE CHARDIN ALBUM the *Church Times* said that Teilhard was a man as lovable and loving as he was intellectually daring and brilliant. We have discussed Teilhard's thought at some length, but in our attempt to give an objective, scientific analysis of it we may have overlooked a very important point. Not only was Teilhard a loving and lovable man, but also his hyperphysics is a theory of love. Love energy animates and directs the whole evolutionary process, and love brings about the final convergence.

Whether or not we understand or accept Teilhard's synthesis, we can and must strive to bring about a further convergence of our species. And this can be brought about only by the truly human energy, that is, truly human love. "If one considers, however briefly, what conditions will make possible the flowering in the human heart of this new universal love, so often vainly dreamed of but now at last leaving the realm of the utopian and declaring itself as both possible and necessary, one notices this: that if men on earth, all over the earth, are ever to love one another it is not enough for them to recognize in one another the elements of a single something; they must also, by developing a 'planetary' consciousness, become aware of the fact that without loss of their individual identities they are becoming a single somebody. For there is no total love—and this is writ large in the gospel—save that which is in and of the personal.

And what does this mean if not that, in the last resort, the 'planetization' of humanity pre-supposes for its proper development not only the contracting of the earth, not only the organizing and condensing of human thought, but also a third factor: the rising on our inward horizon of some psychic cosmic centre, some supreme pole of consciousness, towards which all the elementary consciousnesses of the world shall converge and in which they shall be able to love one another: in other words, the rising of a God."[1]

[1] HYMN OF THE UNIVERSE, p. 89.

# Bibliography

A complete bibliography of Teilhard's works may be found in: Claude Cuénot, TEILHARD DE CHARDIN, A BIOGRAPHICAL STUDY, 1965, Burns Oates. (Original French text, 1958 by Librairie Plon.)

The bibliography below contains the following:
A. The English translations of the works of Teilhard de Chardin (editions used in above text).
B. An annotated bibliography of some of Teilhard's works which are particularly related to topics discussed above.
C. A selection of volumes about the life and thought of Teilhard.
D. A short list of works by other authors, suggested as related reading.

---

# A

THE PHENOMENON OF MAN, London, Collins, 1959, 318pp. Translated by Bernard Wall; introduction by Sir Julian Huxley.

LE MILIEU DIVIN, London, Collins, 1960, 160pp. General edition by Bernard Wall.

LETTERS FROM A TRAVELLER, London, Collins, 1962, 380pp. Translated from LETTRES DE VOYAGE and NOUVELLES LETTRES DE VOYAGE. General editor, Bernard Wall. Introductions by Julian Huxley, Claude Aragonnés and Pierre Leroy.

THE FUTURE OF MAN, London, Collins, 1964, 319pp. Translated by N. Denny.

HYMN OF THE UNIVERSE, London, Collins, 1965, 157pp. Translated by Simon Bartholomew.

LETTERS FROM EGYPT, New York, Herder and Herder, 1965, 256pp. Translated by Mary Ilford.

THE MAKING OF A MIND, London, Collins, 1965, 315pp. Translated from GENÈSE D'UNE PENSÉE by René Hague.

THE APPEARANCE OF MAN, London, Collins, 1965, 286pp. Translated by J. M. Cohen. Preface by Desmond Collins.

THE VISION OF THE PAST, London, Collins, 1966, 285pp. Translated by J. M. Cohen.

MAN'S PLACE IN NATURE, London, Collins, 1966, 127pp. Translated by René Hague.

# B

Teilhard de Chardin, Pierre, "L'Activation de l'Energie Humaine", in L'ACTIVATION DE L'ENERGIE, pp. 407-416. Written in 1953, this is a brief discussion of the two energies: radial (irreversible) and tangential (following the laws of thermodynamics).

"Agitation ou Genèse", in L'AVENIR DE L'HOMME, pp. 273-289. Written in 1947, this essay attempts to show a main axis of evolution, and hence orthogenesis, by showing that life, human reflection, socialization and the Church are not epiphenomena of evolution.

"Barrière de la Mort et Co-Réflexion", in L'ACTIVATION DE L'ENERGIE, pp. 417-429. Written in January 1955, this is a discussion of irreversibility with a comment on the relationship between science and faith.

"Comment Concevoir et Espérer que se Réalise sur Terre l'Unanimisation Humaine?" in L'AVENIR DE L'HOMME, pp. 365-374. Written in 1950, this is a brief explanation of convergence in terms of enforced unification (geographical and mental curvature of compression) and free unification through attraction (love).

"La Convergence de l'Univers" in L'ACTIVATION DE L'ÉNERGIE, pp. 293-309. Written in 1951, this work is especially important for its "lignes d'attaque permettant de vérifier plus outre la réalité du phénomène"—in particular, the convergence of the Noosphere.

"Une Défense de l'Orthogénèse à Propos des Figures de Spéciation", in LA VISION DU PASSÉ, pp. 381-391. Written in January 1955 this is a statement of the scientific necessity of considering evolution in terms of vectors (or orthogenesis), in spite of chance, entropy and the complexity of the lines of evolutionary advance.

"Du Pré-Humain à l'Ultra-Humain", in L'AVENIR DE L'HOMME, pp. 375-385. Written in 1950, this short work contains some important statements on statistical necessity, autogenesis and orthogenesis.

"L'Esprit Nouveau", in L'AVENIR DE L'HOMME, pp. 107-126. An essay written in 1942 in which Teilhard wishes to explain clearly so that all can understand without ambiguity his theory of the convergence of the Noosphere through reflexion and love.

"Evolution Zoologique et Invention," in LA VISION DU PASSÉ, pp. 327-331. Written in 1947, this is a brief presentation of Teilhard's use of the Lamarckian principle of evolution.

"La Fin de l'Espèce", in L'AVENIR DE L'HOMME, pp. 387-395. Written in 1952, this work is important for its discussion of irreversibility based on man's desire for "more-being".

"La Formation de la Noosphère", in L'AVENIR DE L'HOMME, pp. 199-231. Written in 1947 this is, according to Teilhard: "une interprétation biologique plausible de l'Histoire Humaine". It is an explanation of the concept of the Noosphere, its phases, birth, anatomy and the necessary transformation required to escape from entropy. It also contains a definition of orthogenesis, and a comment on Lamarckian evolution in the Noosphere.

"Le Goût de Vivre", in L'ACTIVATION DE L'ENERGIE, pp. 237-251. Written in 1950, this work explains the necessary role of autogenesis in evolution. Autogenesis is presented as a psychic "goût de vivre". This is the basis of Teilhard's Lamarckian principle which is used with Darwinian ectogenesis as an explanation of evolution.

"Un Grand Evénement qui se Dessine: La Planétisation Humaine", in L'AVENIR DE L'HOMME, pp. 157-175. Written in 1945, this is a short essay on the stages of convergence of Man. Planetisation refers to the total reflexion of mankind upon itself.

"Note sur la Réalité Actuelle et la Signification évolutive d'une Orthogénèse Humaine", in LA VISION DU PASSÉ, pp. 351-362. Written in 1951, this is a brief discussion of the acceleration of autogenesis in human development.

"Le Phénomène Humain", in LA VISION DU PASSÉ, pp. 225-243. Written in 1930, this work contains some of Teilhard's earlier views on irreversible development in the light of chance and entropy. These views are basically the same as those presented some twenty years later.

LE PHÉNOMÈNE HUMAIN, Paris, Editions du Seuil, 1955, 348pp. Introduction by N. M. Wildiers. This work, written between June 1938 and June 1940 with some additions and revisions in 1947-48, may be considered to be Teilhard's most important single work. It is based on his matured world-vision and presents an extensive account of his whole phenomenology, or hyperphysics, as well as his concept of "Christogenesis". It should not, however, be looked upon as a complete or intensive development of his theory. A complete understanding of LE PHÉNOMÈNE HUMAIN could come only within the context of Teilhard's many other works on this theme. Such is certainly the case with his theories of orthogenesis and autogenesis which are not fully developed in this work.

LA PLACE DE L'HOMME DANS LA NATURE, Paris, Editions du Seuil, 1963, 173pp. Republished from: LE GROUPE ZOOLOGIQUE HUMAIN, Paris, Editions Albin Michel, 1956, xiii + 172pp. Written in 1950 this work is a study of the evolutionary structure and directions of the human zoological group. It contains chapters on the development of living matter, the biosphere, Man, the expansion of the Noosphere and the compression of the Noosphere. It closely parallels LE PHÉNOMÈNE HUMAIN, but contains more technical or scientific data.

"La Place de l'Homme dans l'Univers", in LA VISION DE PASSÉ, pp. 303-321. Written in 1942 this work contains Teilhard's concept of the "trois infinis" and man's position in the universe relative to them. It also contains a brief statement on his criterion for truth.

"Le Rebondissement Humain de l'Evolution et ses Conséquences", in L'AVENIR DE L'HOMME, pp. 251-271. Written in 1947 this is an analysis of the Noosphere with some emphasis on Darwinian and Lamarckian evolution, autogenesis and ectogenesis, and design and chance.

"La Réflexion de l'Energie", in L'ACTIVATION DE L'ENERGIE, pp. 333-353. Written in 1952, this essay explains the future first in terms of the law of entropy, and then in terms of the transformation necessary for the irreversibility of reflexion.

"Réflexions sur le Progrès", in L'AVENIR DE L'HOMME, pp. 83-106. Written in 1941, this is an essay in two parts: I, "L'Avenir de l'Homme vu par un Paléontologiste". II, "Sur les Bases Possibles d'un Credo Humain Commun." It presents an optimistic view of the future based, according to Teilhard, on scientific reasons, and develops the concept of a converging noosphere.

"Les Singularités de l'Espèce Humaine," in L'APPARITION DE L'HOMME, pp. 293-374. Written in 1954, this work presents Teilhard's explanation of the development of the Noosphere in terms of its convergence and co-reflexion. Entropy is presented as one of two currents of evolution, the second being "complexity-consciousness". The latter continues through a separation of radial energy from tangential energy.

"La Structure Phylétique du Groupe Humain", in L'APPARITION DE L'HOMME, pp. 185-242. Written in 1951, this work contains important material on the existence of a principal axis of evolution and the extension of this axis into the future. In it Teilhard's views of chance, entropy, transformation of the Noosphere and the meaning of orthogenesis are clarified.

"Sur la Loi d'Irréversibilité en Evolution", in LA VISION DU PASSÉ, pp. 71-74. This is a brief work, written in 1923, defining and distinguishing irreversibility and orthogenesis.

"Sur les Degrés de Certitude Scientifique de l'Idée d'Evolution", in SCIENCE ET CHRIST, pp. 245-249. This brief work, written in 1947 contains some comment on the two energies.

"Sur l'Existence Probable, En Avant de Nous, d'un 'Ultra-Humain'," in L'AVENIR DE L'HOMME, pp. 351-364. Written in 1950, this is a brief extrapolation from a "physico-biological definition" of man to the convergence of the Noosphere.

"Transformations et Prolongements en l'Homme du Mécanisme de l'Evolution" in L'ACTIVATION DE L'ENERGIE, pp. 311-332. Written in 1951 for Sir Julian Huxley, this essay explains convergence in terms of the mechanism of autoevolution.

"Vie et Planètes" in L'AVENIR DE L'HOMME, pp. 127-156. Written in 1946, this lecture contains a discussion of the "chance birth" of our planet, its significance as the source of life, and an important statement on the transformation which will free converging mankind from the law of entropy.

"La Vision du Passé" in LA VISION DU PASSÉ, pp. 333-343. Written in 1949 this work contains a brief discussion of orthogenesis and the "privileged axis" of evolution.

# C

**Barjon, Louis** and **Leroy, Pierre,** LA CARRIERE SCIENTIFIQUE DE PIERRE TEILHARD DE CHARDIN, Monaco, Editions de Rocher, 1964, 140pp.

**Barthelemy-Madaule, Madeleine,** BERGSON ET TEILHARD DE CHARDIN, Paris, Editions du Seuil, 1963, 686pp. This comparison between Bergson and Teilhard contains a general exposition of Teilhard's synthesis, including sections on orthogenesis, the two energies, finality and the nature of Teilhard's synthesis.

**Blanchard, J. P.,** MÉTHODE ET PRINCIPES DU PÈRE TEILHARD DE CHARDIN, Paris, La Colombe, 1961, 190pp. This work is a demonstration, in Teilhardian terms, that science can and must lead to God, and through God to Christ. It contains some criticism of Teilhard's method, especially of his use of analogy.

**Chauchard, Paul,** LA PENSÉE SCIENTIFIQUE DE TEILHARD, Paris, Editions Universitaires, 1965, 270pp. The author tries to show the scientific aspect of all of Teilhard's work.

**Cuénot, Claude,** NOUVEAU LEXIQUE TEILHARD DE CHARDIN, Paris, Editions du Seuil, 1968, 223pp.

PIERRE TEILHARD DE CHARDIN, LES GRANDES ETAPES DE SON EVOLUTION, Paris, Plon, 1958, 489 + LIIIpp. This is an excellent biography of Teilhard with an analysis of his thought development. Many quotations from Teilhard are used. Contains the most complete bibliography of Teilhard's works to date. English translation: TEILHARD DE CHARDIN, translated by V. Colimore, edited by R. Hague, Baltimore, London, Burns & Oates, 1965, vi + 492pp.

TEILHARD DE CHARDIN, Paris, Editions du Seuil, 1962, 191pp. Contains texts of Teilhard with commentaries, biography, bibliography and vocabulary.

SCIENCE AND FAITH IN TEILHARD DE CHARDIN, London, Garnstone Press, 1967, 112pp.; with a Comment by Roger Garaudy (Volume 1 of "The Teilhard Study Library"; General Editors: Bernard Towers and Anthony Dyson).

**Cuypers, Hubert,** POUR OU CONTRE TEILHARD, Paris, Editions Universitaires, 1962 (Volume 4 of "Carnets Teilhard") 59pp.— includes brief criticisms of Teilhard's science, philosophy and theology.

VOCABULAIRE TEILHARD, Paris, Editions Universitaires, 1963 (Volumes 5 and 6 of "Carnets Teilhard")—a lexicon of Teilhardian terminology with references to his works.

**Francoeur, Robert T.** (editor), THE WORLD OF TEILHARD, Baltimore, Helicon Press, 1961, 208pp. A general critique and analysis of Teilhard's world by scientists, philosophers, psychologists, theologians, etc. such as Weigel, Stern, Barbour and Bruns.

**Grenet, Paul,** TEILHARD DE CHARDIN, THE MAN AND HIS THEORIES, translated by R. A. Rudorft, London, Souvenir Press, 1965, 176pp.— contains biography and some discussion of Teilhard as a scientist, theologian and philospher. Also contains some selected writings of Teilhard.

**Grenet, Paul-Bernard,** PIERRE TEILHARD DE CHARDIN OU LE PHILO-SOPHE MALGRÉ LUI, Paris, Beauchesne, 1960, 258pp. A critique of Teilhard's "philosophy" with specific sections on the "weakness" of his concept of The All, of his use of analogy, of his notion of novelty, of his concepts of matter and spirit, and of his notion of being.

**Magloire, George** and **Cuypers, Hubert,** PRÉSENCE DE PIERRE TEILHARD DE CHARDIN, Paris, Editions Universitaires, 1961, 226pp. Contains a biography of Teilhard and an analysis of his thought; also a lexicon and bibliography.

**Rabut, Oliver,** DIALOGUE WITH TEILHARD DE CHARDIN, London, Sheed and Ward, 1961, 247pp. This is a critique of Teilhard, mainly from a scientific viewpoint. It contains interesting comments on Teilhard's methods, his use of the theory of evolution, his panpsychism and his concept of the two energies.

**Rideau, Emile,** TEILHARD DE CHARDIN; A GUIDE TO HIS THOUGHT, London, Collins, 1967, 672pp. This is a very complete account of Teilhard's synthesis containing some material on all of the main topics considered in this volume.

**Towers, Bernard,** TEILHARD DE CHARDIN, London, The Carey Kingsgate Press Ltd., 1966, 45pp. An excellent introduction to Teilhard's life, thought and the significance of his work.

**Towers, Bernard** and **Dyson, Anthony** (General Editors), EVOLUTION, MARXISM AND CHRISTIANITY, London, Garnstone Press, 1967, 116pp. (Volume 2 of "The Teilhard Study Library"). Essays by C. Cuénot, F. G. Elliott, R. Garaudy, A. O. Dyson, P. G. Fothergill and B. Towers.

**Thys, Albert,** CONSCIENCE-RÉFLEXION COLLECTIVISATION CHEZ TEILHARD, Paris, Editions Universitaires, 1964, 127pp. (Volumes 15 and 16 of "Carnets Teilhard".) This is an analysis of Teilhard's theory of the development of consciousness and the noosphere.

**Tresmontant, Claude,** INTRODUCTION A LA PENSÉE DE TEILHARD DE CHARDIN, Paris, Editions du Seuil, 1956, 134pp. English translation: PIERRE TEILHARD DE CHARDIN, HIS THOUGHT, translated by S. Attanasio, Baltimore, Helicon Press, 1959, viii + 128pp. This is a general introduction to Teilhard's thought, containing a good analysis of his principle of coherence, autoevolution and the nature of his works.

# D

**Blum, Harold F.,** TIME'S ARROW AND EVOLUTION, New York, Harper Torchbook, 1962, x + 220pp. This work is especially important for its considerations of evolution in relation to the second law of thermodynamics.

**Bohm, David,** CAUSALITY AND CHANCE IN MODERN PHYSICS, New York, Harper Torchbook, 1961, xi + 170pp. Foreword by Louis de Broglie. This is an excellent work on chance, design, probability, statistical laws, mechanism and related topics within the context of modern physical science.

**Dobzhansky, Theodosius,** MANKIND EVOLVING, New Haven, Yale University Press, 1962, xiii + 381pp. This is an excellent study of man as the product of evolution by one of the world's leading zoo-logists. It contains some discussion on orthogenesis, autogenesis, and irreversibility, and concludes with a brief comment on the thought of Teilhard.

**Huxley, Sir Julian,** EVOLUTION IN ACTION, New York, New American Library of World Literature, 1957, viii + 141pp. In the light of evolutionary theory Huxley explores the future possibilities of man. This work contains a good general explanation of the modern theory of evolution as well as the author's own humanistic approach. Also there is some discussion of orthogenesis and the "vital force".

**Simpson, George Gaylord,** THE MEANING OF EVOLUTION, New York, The New American Library of World Literature Inc., 1956, 192pp. A general explanation of evolutionary theory by a leading paleonto-logist, this work discusses orthogenesis, the forces of evolution and other topics related to this work.

**Tax, Sol** (editor), EVOLUTION AFTER DARWIN, Chicago, The University of Chicago Press, 1960. This is a three volume work based on the Darwin Centennial Celebration held at the University of Chicago. Vol. I, THE EVOLUTION OF LIFE: ITS ORIGIN, HISTORY AND FUTURE, viii + 629pp. Vol. II, THE EVOLUTION OF MAN: MIND, CULTURE AND SOCIETY, viii + 473pp. Vol. III, ISSUES IN EVOLUTION: THE UNIVERSITY OF CHICAGO CENTENNIAL DISCUSSIONS, viii + 310pp. This is an excellent collection of articles on all aspects of evolution by today's leading authorities. The accounts of the panel discussions in Vol. III are of particular interest.

**Waddington, C. H.,** THE NATURE OF LIFE, New York, Atheneum, 1962, 131pp. This excellent work discusses many problems related to evolution, including the difference between life and non-life, purpose and man's freedom.

# Index Of Names